IT OPENS ON A RUBBISH TIP that doubles for a training ground littered with refuse engineers - known in those distant pre-politically correct days of 30 years ago as dustmen - and ends, more or less, at Elland Road, home of Leeds United and the European Cup finalists the previous season. The diaries of David McVay, written during his formative years as a teenager with Notts County during the 1970s, invite readers on an undulating and nostalgic soccer sojourn that can never be repeated in the context of the modern game.

McVay's jottings create an evocative tapestry of a bygone and almost innocent age for football and his contemporary observations and insights deftly portray the decade that style forgot but one which still gives a generation sleepless nights.

From February 1974 to October 1975, the scenery varies from The Shay at Halifax to Old Trafford while the cast of characters includes such luminaries as Don Revie and Brian Clough; the Ford Capri and Cortina provide the car chases with background music courtesy of assorted artists such as Slade, Yes and Nick Drake. Of course nobody takes the credit for the wardrobe or dress sense director.

On the pitch, Manchester United visit Meadow Lane and their fans almost destroy it as Jimmy Sirrel, the Notts County manager whose marvellous idiosyncrasies illuminate the book, repels the Mancunian hordes with a bunion scalpel.

Off it, Paul Smith opens his first boutique in the backstreets of Nottingham (his prices have risen steadily since) while the Exorcist and Abba arrive in equally garish manner.

Steak...Diana Ross; Diary of a Football Nobody celebrates with candid humour the team ethic and provincial camaraderie that was endemic in the sport long before the foreign legions invaded. The drink was always strong but the women stronger as a raw and diverse mixture of combustible personalities, thrown together into the community of the dr-- - room, strived desperately to wir
despite a hectic social calendar.

D1642739

STEAK... DIANA ROSS

Diary of a Football Nobody

David McVay

The Parrs Wood Press
MANCHESTER

First Published 2003

THE PARRS WOOD PRESS
St Wilfrid's Enterprise Centre
Royce Road, Manchester, M15 5BJ
www.parrswoodpress.com

ISBN: 1 903158 37 0

Printed by:

FOTOLITO LONGO s.p.a.
Bolzano
Italy

For William McVay (1901-1975) - often recalled the day he saw Workington Reds take a one-goal lead against Manchester United's Busby Babes at Borough Park in the FA Cup. A great football fan and grandfather to whom I never did say goodbye.

Arthur Mann (1948-1999) - the friendliest of colleagues and a tower of strength in some of my darker hours at Meadow Lane. God bless Archie.

My son Tom who is old enough now to know that I was not the David Beckham of my day while my daughter Jessica, for the moment, will love me all the same even if I played like Victoria Beckham. My grateful thanks to them and my wife Debby, a great solace to me while enduring some late nights burning the midnight oil trying to complete this task from Bunny to Florida.

Acknowledgements to the library staff at the Nottingham Evening Post and Mick Holland for his advice and invaluable help.

FOREWORD

by Billy Ivory
(screenwriter, Notts County fan and creator of the
acclaimed television drama 'Common As Muck')

MCVAY'S STORY is an extraordinary one. Or an ordinary one. Depending upon when you were born and whether you remember the days when team kit tended only to be worn by the eleven poor buggers out in the middle, desperately trying to survive a waterlogged pitch and the cruelty of a five thousand gate.

It is the story of a star, nevertheless, a man who was looked up to (by me, among others) but for whom the current heady days of massive salaries, celebrity status and TV presenter girlfriends was all but a dream.

McVay played his soccer in the nineteen-seventies, for Notts County amongst others, when players were still of the people...elevated, true, but still inhabiting the same world, as he ruefully remembers when describing his salutary bus journeys home to Clifton in Notts with some of the late returning crowd - not all of whom approved of the young colt's performance.

The book is desperately funny and sad too. McVay writes beautifully about his family and the difficulties of adapting to the "dream" existence as a young soccer player (in his case) very much concerned with life beyond the pitch.

Above all though, the book is comedy. The best kind...the kind that makes beer shoot down your nose when an unexpected sentence pokes you violently in the ribs.

For the Notts County team of Jimmy Sirrel, which McVay forced his way into, reveals itself a rogue's gallery, par excellence. Make no mistake, these lads could play: they made it to the old First Division in no time, but they had other talents too. And boy could they drink, swear, fight, skive, feign injury, incite riot and above all indulge in post-match leg-overs the likes of which would these days result in six weeks on the physio's table and a cruciate ligament op.

And that's the thing about Diary of a Football No-Body...Though it recalls a time when players got less - less money, less deification from the crowds, less of everything handed to them on a plate, perversely, they also got more. Because that closeness to their roots, that awareness that they were only a bus ride away from standing in the crowd, never mind strutting their stuff before it, made these lads behave as you or I might if we were told that next week we were running out for the city's first eleven...they filled their boots, unable to believe their luck.

Which is the real joy of McVay's story. These boys aren't cool, well-behaved ambassadors of the game, looking to elevate soccer to a position up there with medicine and law in the career pantheon. No, this is Johnny Rotten, Sid Vicious and the rest in shorts and a pair of shinnies. This is Banzai soccer; what we all know the beautiful game to really be about deep down: passion, excess and overload; hungry lads let loose in a sweetshop where moments before they had their noses hard pressed against the window. And then when you're buggered you stop. Brilliant.

INTRODUCTION

SHORTLY BEFORE John Barnwell became manager of Notts County in 1987, I was introduced to the former Nottingham Forest and Arsenal player in one of the club's many bars (funny how the Meadow Lane ground always seemed to have more beer pumps than players) in my capacity as reporter for the Nottingham Evening Post. "I remember you David, of course I do. Hope you can write better than you could play." Well he did once share a flat with Ronnie Corbett in his playing days so I suppose the sense of humour was to be expected.

There were really only two things I did marginally better than other subjects at school - they were writing and playing football. That the latter should form the first ten years of my working life was largely due to a degree of talent and a fair share of good fortune. Not wishing to abandon totally any scholastic ability that a variety of excellent and patient teachers had imbued in me during my seven years at Fairham Comprehensive School, I decided to keep a regular diary of events from the day I left that notorious seat of learning on Clifton Estate.

That was July 1973 and my efforts lasted until the pen and inspiration ran out; it was early in 1976 that the diaries were abandoned because of a lager-logged brain and an incurable bout of apathy.

Before embarking on this project, I had dusted down the old diaries and re-read each one, page after relentless page, and thought: "What a bloody boring life I must have led then to have sat down each night and tried to express in words that day's events." Still, in hindsight I am rather pleased that I took the trouble even if some of the scribblings were like myself, much the worse for wear and almost impossible to decipher at the end of a long day and punishing night.

Not that I will pass them on to my younger generation as a testament to the decade or a social document of that period of time. There are far too many personal and far too many irrelevant and frankly self-indulgent references among those idle jottings to deem them worthy of revealing fully to anyone other than myself.

But in the midst of it all, there are some shining examples of the characters of that time and the general approach to training and matches in professional football that was prevalent nearly thirty years ago; people and places that illuminated and played such a large part of my life back then and, to a smaller degree, the lives of thousands of Notts County supporters.

It is an era not just of football that can never return but also a society and its attitudes, too. The game was, by today's standards, impoverished but nevertheless it was beautiful - well, now and again at any rate. Reading the diaries in full once more certainly revived memories - some painful, some awkward and some poignant balanced by some happy and joyous ones too. Safe to say, that's a fair reflection of many of our lives trying to grow up while coming to terms with platform shoes and Slade in the 1970s.

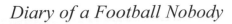
Thursday, February 28, 1974

The colour red is prominent in thoughts today. On Sunday we're playing Nottingham Forest, the evil slime from across the River Trent. But today is also General Election Day and for a lad brought up on Europe's largest council housing estate the choices are simple - Labour or Labour Reserves.

It's a tricky one to call. The Labour candidate for the Nottingham Central constituency is none other than Jack Dunnett, illustrious chairman of Notts County FC. An MP who has chalked up more appearances in Private Eye than he has in the House of Commons. How in all conscience can you vote Labour knowing it will elect JD?

No matter. First comes training at Wilford Tip, just a five minute car ride from Meadow Lane. The local council likes to unload refuse on part of this vast area of flat and unprotected land. When the wind blows across from the Trent at least the dustbinmen get an unexpected laugh watching us try to control the ball in one of the thousands of practice matches we stage up there.

10.30am: Let play commence. The gaffer blows his whistle for practice match No. 22 - this month. After five minutes I trap a loose ball almost apologetically. This isn't in the script, the 'Chosen one', that is me, knows it. The gaffer almost freaks trying to get the whistle, tied by thick string around his elbow, to his lips before I can pass it forward.

"Jesus Christ you're playing son. But you're not really playing, aye." Jimmy Sirrel's guttural Glaswegian defies comprehension at the best of times but when he talks in tartan riddles - Jesus! I know my place. I am to stick to reserve striker Mick Vinter's yellow bib and posterior like sheep droppings on a shagpile. The game progresses around me. We could be losing 10-0 to the bloody reserves, the Martians can land on Wilford Tip but I am blissfully unaware of it all. The Vint must be stopped, at all costs.

On Sunday, it will be a red shirt not a yellow bib and the posterior will belong to Duncan McKenzie. He's earned rave reviews in Forest's FA Cup run this season. Watching him play at the City Ground recently, clearly he's got the odd trick or two but I think the gaffer is slightly overestimating his talents.

At the end of an hour, 30 minutes each way, I'm severely pissed off. It's not in a footballer's nature to play this way, boss. My natural instinct is to follow the ball, boss, keep up with play, boss. And tackle more than just one member of the opposition - boss.

"Don't worry David. You're playing but you're not playing son." Aaargh.

I don't know who is more pissed off. Me, Vint or the dustbinmen making an early delivery across the fields.

Vint's particularly peeved. "What am I, your bloody stooge or something? I'm just running around pretending to be frigging Duncan McKenzie. What the effing hell use is that to me."

He had a point. Vint's a year older than me and should be knocking on the first team door more regularly. He scores a lot of goals in the Stiffs but with Les Bradd and Kevin Randall up front he just can't get a look in. I sympathise. I feel slightly ashamed that he should be waiting in the wings while I, a late starter who left school with three A levels the previous summer, should have been chosen so quickly for better things. It's a burden I carry with the rest of the younger players. They've all cleaned a thousand boots, swept the icy terraces in winter and painted the wooden stands in summer as apprentices. Meanwhile I've sat A levels and learned how to say 'thank you' in Russian.

So what have I done so special to leap ahead of them in the pecking order? If the younger pros don't exude resentment, it's to their credit. But at times I feel so damn guilty, almost like a silver spoon has been belatedly handed to me.

Despite the first team status, I still change in the 'reserve' dressing room along with most of the other young pros. In the shower room, Ian Bolton assesses his day. Smoke from his third filter tip of the morning (two before training) shrouds the giant concrete communal bath.

"Where you going then Vint? Not home to the missus again? Fancy a game of snooker up by the theatre? Come on, Vint."

Under peer pressure, Vint agrees. By 1pm Bernie (the Bolt) has consumed several bacon butties at the cafe on the corner of the ground and is well on the way to his second 10-pack of Rothmans. Over 100 fags or 100 yards nobody at the club can match him for speed.

The day is finished for me. Training has been crap. I've been crap and I feel wholly unwanted and unaccepted amongst the lower ranks.

Time to vote. In previous years some of the senior pros, Bradd, John 'Billy' Brindley and Mick Jones, have been enlisted to drive pensioners to the polling stations on Mr Dunnett's behalf. Great tactics using popular local lads made goodish to promote the socialist image. A kiss of the baby's head at the local miners' institute (the Stoot) usually confirms his love of the working classes.

Even so, the dire choices are Jolly Jack or the crew member representing the sailor Grocer Heath. Eventually 'X' marks the spot next to the Labour candidate, this time for Nottingham East. Somewhere, not too far away, somebody is voting for Mr JACK DUNNETT (Lab).

No wonder I feel so bloody guilty.

Saturday, March 2

The trusty Fiat 128 (£650, white, 'K' reg, and a rust-free Italian motor car) takes me to the Posthouse at Sandiacre, a few miles outside the city centre. Not nervous about tomorrow's match but like all derby games, the incentive to win is much greater when you've got to show your face in the city the following day.

The Nottingham derby is perhaps unique in football - unique because the rival fans are not driven at all by passion or religious divides. In the case of County fans, they are driven by 'the green-eyed monster that lurks inside us all' (knew that A level English Lit would come in handy). Sheer unbridled jealousy. You can understand why.

In the 1950s Notts fans had Tommy Lawton packing them in at Meadow Lane, 50,000 or more every other week. Unquestionably County were the talk of the town and top dogs in the city. But in 1959 Forest won the FA

Cup and before you could blink the 1960s were upon us in a flash, brash and psychedelic fashion. First Division Forest's 'fancy dans' fitted the decade perfectly with young stars like Ian Storey-Moore and Henry Newton enticing a new generation of supporters to the City Ground where the Trent End chanted Zigga-Zagga Zigga-Zagga Joe Baker. The England centre forward became a local legend alongside Robin Hood. Even the team ran out to the theme tune of the television series about the man in Lincoln Green.

Over at Meadow Lane, spectators couldn't tell which was suffering most from dry rot - the main stand or the players. The drab, old fashioned black and white striped shirts reflected the club's fall from grace to the bottom of the Fourth Division. An old order refusing to accept change watched by a dwindling faithful who were either disenchanted or deceased.

Now, with the two clubs back on a par, it's payback time. At least it is for Notts fans who had suffered for more than a decade the humiliation of a far too cocky and loud neighbour and the ignominy of supporting a team that kept a cluster of east coast comedians in gags and employment for several winter seasons at Skegness, Mablethorpe and Chapel-St Leonards.

The responsibility falls heavy on the shoulders of Bradd and Brindley. The sense of history is not lost on them.

8.45pm and both are having a pint at the hotel bar when I arrive.

"Medicinal, McVay. To help us sleep." Since the two are sharing a room and with intimate knowledge of their

liquid capacity, several more firkins will be needed before either arrive in the land of Nod but tonight they will retire after just the one.

I'm rooming with Kevin Randall, otherwise 'The Claw'. Kevin has reached veteran status and knows he'll soon be leaving County. He's scored all his goals (hundreds of them) in the lower reaches and if the club is truly to progress to Division One, it will be without the likes of him.

This doesn't worry him. His value on the transfer market is about £10,000 to £15,000 and he reasons he'll get a 'couple of grand' written into his contract with a new club. He wants one, maybe two more moves to help ease the financial burden when he retires. Brindley, Bradd, Stubbs, there are plenty more in our side who have reached a certain age and status. Christ, I'm 19 this Tuesday. Retirement, family security and long-term plans rank alongside love and marriage as big issues in my life just now.

Kevin's a pro who loves the game, loves scoring and, being a Mancunian, loves talking. At football he played for Chesterfield and Bury in his heyday but he should have represented England at conversation.

The Claw (his nickname derives from going past young defenders then grabbing hold of their shoulders, hair or ears to increase the speed and velocity of his ageing legs) is on good form. Virtually sleep talking. But it keeps me from thinking about tomorrow's showdown with Vint's alter ego, Duncan McKenzie.

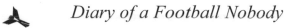

Sunday, March 3

Up early, The Claw is no longer talking. Breakfast boiled egg and toast. About 11.30am, pre-match meal. The usual, rare steak, no sauce. Hang around best part of three hours in the hotel before setting off for Nottingham. Park car at Meadow Lane then 'coach' the half a mile across Trent Bridge to the City Ground. Still, the two card schools have plenty of time to gamble away the next win bonus.

Forest's visitors' dressing room is familiar territory for most of the senior professionals whose spare room cardboard boxes are crammed full of loser's medals in the County Cup over the years (the only other professional side in Nottinghamshire who can contest this prestigious trophy is Mansfield Town).

The steak and boiled egg begin to repeat. I feel an urgent need for the toilet. Billy tells me Stanley Matthews used to throw up down the loo before vital games to get himself down to his fighting weight.

"It's no use Bill," I tell him, attempting a more orthodox method of losing a few pounds sitting in the men's room. I am a fat bastard. Even my own fans tell me this. Shedding a slither of boiled egg yoke will not persuade me or anyone else otherwise.

Stubbo, our hard man centre half, enters Trap 2 for a final fag before kick-off.

The warm up is complete.

Forest still have an outside chance of promotion from Division Two. We've still got a decent chance of relegation. It's essential we don't lose this game. The atmosphere is tense, expectant, nearly 30,000 in the ground. Five minutes to go; a few token stretches, jogging on the spot and we are ready. From kick-off I wander over to McKenzie, a player I've never even spoken to. In the hierarchy of football, you tend to avoid the superstars - or is it, they avoid ungainly youths of no fixed talent?

Forest are playing 4-4-2 trying to get the ball forward to feet as quickly as possible, stylish stuff they've been doing since the days of Imlach, Wilson and Le Flem in the 1950s and '60s. In contrast we've got big Braddy up front, trying to contact him via the airways south of the River Trent, something County teams have been doing since Lawton's era. Such a pity, really, because this City Ground pitch is one of the best surfaces in the country.

The game, though, falls into the Twilight Zone. Eric Probert, Arthur Mann shut down the supply route to the front men. John Robertson and Ian Bowyer aren't getting time to exert their considerable talents on the game. For a quarter of an hour, nothing happens, literally. The crowd is silent, not baying or taunting, more dozing off after a good Sunday lunch.

"For Christ's sake David, get a fucking tackle in on him." It is Don Masson; Masson the Miserable, Masson the Merciless, our leader. He's right, of course. Despite being a most obnoxious piece of work and about as popular as a turd arising in the communal bath, he's absolutely effing right.

Must clobber the flash bastard. Supposed to man-to-man mark him and haven't even seen his backside yet. The game's just passing me by. Come on, get a grip. Here's the ball, there's McKenzie - whack. That was easy.

NOTTINGHAM FOREST
versus
NOTTS. COUNTY

The Official Programme of Nottingham Forest Football Club

SUNDAY, 3rd MARCH, 1974   Kick-off 3 p.m.

7p

"Well done Davie. Well fucking done son. That's fucking better, eh." Masson the Merciless has passed judgement. I have pleased our leader. I feel 10ft tall. McKenzie looks hurt as if to say: "Who the hell are you to kick me you fat bastard?"

9

I don't care. Today, the Notts County shirt seems a little loose and baggy.

Confidence soars. My peers are happy. Perhaps this man-marking game isn't so bad after all.

I'd settle for 0-0 here. But then you don't have to be a rocket scientist to work that one out. We've got five at the back. In fact there are more people in our half of the pitch than there were in Workington's main stand yesterday (half of them would be my bloody relatives). We'll be lucky to get nil although wouldn't you know it, Masson goes close with a bit of magic in the first half.

Half time, Jimmy: Keep it going, eh. Jack Wheeler, our veteran physio, pitches in with his mellow Brummie accent. Keep it going boys. Jimmy again. Chuke them up Brian (Stubbs). David (Needham) you've got to fucking chuke these boys up. Ronnie Fenton, 'yes man' coach has his say (summing up all his powers of original thought with nauseous Geordie twang): Keep it going, lads.

52 minutes: Corner, right side. First tangible action of the afternoon. Forest have stepped up a gear. It's swung in. Everyone's marked, but then Bowyer pops up with a late run on the six yard box - shit, all that good work. But somehow Eric McManus, our Irish goalie, palms it over. Supermac! Bloody fantastic, you Irish git. Brilliant, you Paddy bastard. Masson the horrible takes Mac's earlobe off thundering his verbal gratitude. The boys are generous and genuine in their praise.

Minutes later, as Forest push forward I take the ball effortlessly off McKenzie and stroke it back to Eric. Applause, even from the Forest fans. A rush of adrenalin, Forest attack down the left, a low cross, McKenzie's boot lunges, my head intercepts - ball and boot. Even his famed flick trick isn't working.

It finishes goalless. "Today, you grew up a little eh son - aye well maybe, eh David." Jimmy's on his first tot of whisky. Stubbo has joined him. But the day has just begun.

Monday, March 4

It's late afternoon. The body is willing but the head is quite stubborn. Reflect on yesterday's events after the game. Back to car park, drive down to London for the first Professional Footballers' Association awards dinner at the Hilton Hotel, Park Lane.

Change in to monkey suit at hotel in Kensington. Bradd and Brindley realise the momentous occasion. Already in hotel bar having a pint as we arrive in lobby. "What kept you?" I had Masson the Merciful and Needham in my car on the drive down the M1.

Off to Hilton. Explore a little. 8pm: Discover Billy Wright and Tommy Docherty in lift. Conversation going down, on Flowerpot Men level. Bill: Flobadob, flobadob. Ben (alias Tommy): Flobadob, Billy, och aye flobabigdob Billy. Weed, as in urine, certain to pop up soon. Leave them on third floor still searching for the right buttons to press.

Ceremony begins around 9pm. Sat at front table. Jolly Jack, our newly elected Labour MP, dutifully celebrates by buying two crates of bottled pale ale for the table. What a man of the people.

Dickie Davies introduces the awards to television. Masson and McKenzie make divisional awards team.

MAGPIES' TACTICS UNDER FIRE FROM BROWN

By JOHN LAWSON

NOTTS. County's defensive attitude in yesterday's City derby was still being attacked today by Nottingham Forest's management and fans.

And City Ground manager Allan Brown led the critics when he declared: "If you have not got the players with quality you have got to think of other ways of winning and that's just what they did.

COVERING

"I would have thought they would have looked at their place in the table and said let's have a go and try and win. But they just did not want to know and we all saw the result.

One of the big talking points afterwards was the performance of young David McVay in subduing Forest's potential match winger Duncan McKenzie but Brown refused to acknowledge the fact.

He said "It's rubbish to say that McVay played Duncan out of the game. There were several times when he got past him but we had so few players marking it was difficult to find a way through.

It's easy to surrender midfield and let teams come at you if you can park your defence as Notts did.

But we did have chances, though, and if that shot of Ian Bowyer's had gone in everyone would have said we deserved to win."

But as far as Forest are concerned the inglorious derby is now a mere statistic in the record books.

It's all go for Saturday's sixth round Cup clash at Newcastle and Brown is left with selection problems on which to deliberate this week.

The form of John Robertson in his comeback game might well have won the 21 year old Scot a place in the side.

"John used the ball well and showed us the quality he has got." said Brown. "It's only his fitness that has been in doubt until yesterday — nothing else."

REQUEST

Brown, however, revealed today that Robertson would probably have been left out had it not been for Martin O'Neill wanting to play with the reserves at Stoke on Saturday.

"If Martin had been in the party he would have played yesterday," said Brown who on Saturday agreed to a transfer request from Forest's unhappy 22-year-old Irish international midfield man.

Crowds up on angry Sunday

Sunday soccer continued to draw the big crowds ye...

DAVE McVAY...under orders to shadow McKenzie

The morning after the afternoon ahead of the night before.

The Nottingham derby delayed serious drinking on the way to the first PFA Awards Dinner at the London Hilton. Our tactics, aimed to get the game over quickly and thus extend drinking hours, were condemned by Allan Brown, the Forest manager, in the local Evening Post.

My hero Denis Law wins special trophy for services to football. He's also The Claw's hero.

Awards over, The Claw and I lurk with schoolboy intent to get the great man's autograph. Neither of us can pluck up courage. My excuse: I'm nearly drunk and nearly 19. The Claw: He's 50 going on 70 and isn't man enough to thrust a menu in the Lawman's face and ask 'Sign please - it's for my grandchildren.' Bastard.

The biggest shock of the night still to come. £1.50 for a Bacardi and Coke! Jesus Christ.

Even now, can't quite recall the previous night. Somehow ended in the Playboy Club up the road, signed in by Tommy Docherty. Me, at the Playboy Club. Girls with fluffy tails, Arabs with fluffy towels around their heads and £1,000 chips (that's a lot of Bacardi and a substantial amount of Coke). Christ I'm bladdered. Is this Ken Russell's version of the Nativity Play with lecherous, gambling shepherds having exchanged their woolly flock for a warren-full of bloody nubile rabbits?

And there's Brindley - at least I think it is he - risking the last £5 of our kitty on the red coming up. This really isn't happening to a lad from Clifton Estate.

Tuesday, March 5

Life's three great lies. Miners don't strike, David Cassidy shaves, I promise I'll drive you home afterwards and oh, the fourth, footballers don't read match reports in the newspapers.

Catch up with yesterday's news. Mr Clough, the Derby County manager, reckons that if McKenzie is worth £200,000, how much is McVay worth? In the local paper, the Forest reporter writes that if McKenzie caught the train to the PFA awards, I would have been sitting in the compartment next to him on the journey down to St Pancras.

On my 19th birthday, I feel good. As Brindley would say, you're only a prawn in the game, McVay, but the

world could be your oyster sauce. Then, as a rule, he'd fall off the bar stool.

Wednesday, March 6

If medals were awarded for honesty, decency and for being a downright good egg Andy Beattie would need a room the size of Meadow Lane to display his silverware. The man who signed Denis Law when he was manager of Huddersfield Town, he is a scout with Notts and just one of the nicest blokes I ever met during my admittedly limited time in what I reckon is the rat race of football. He asked to see me after training and we had a long and frank chat. I told him that I wasn't sure if I was still enjoying my football, that I was thinking of packing it up and going to college or something and he listened and gave his point of view. He told me to carry on playing and study part-time. "Keep playing while you are young and healthy," he said. I must apply for college next year and start doing something with my afternoons instead of idling the time away doing shit all. Can't see me standing behind the bar of the local pub smiling to customers seven days a week.

Succumbed to a quick post-training pint in the Lion on Clumber Street. Introduced to Tommy Lawton, the old England centre forward, who was holding court with a motley crew of creeps and spongers. Downing pints of bitter as if it was going out of fashion followed by whisky chasers, he looked rather shabby and pathetic in their company.

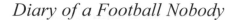 # Thursday, March 7

As arranged, Brindley gives me a lift and arrives at our family home in Clifton (council semi, three bedrooms, five adults, two left home and another trying his damnedest to get away). Training starts at 10 am and it's only 20 minutes' drive to the ground but I'm dragged out of bed at 8.30am. He's on his bloody egg round. Off in the traditional puff of smoke in his red Hillman Hunter, the clutch clinging on for dear life and he's taking three dozen fresh bloody eggs to a pub in Beeston, over the River Trent and in the opposite direction from where we need to be. 'Billy' is what we call one of the game's characters. "McVay, there are no characters left in the game . . .all bloody gone" he tells me as we cross the Trent via Clifton Bridge. Meadows-born and bred is Billy. The Meadows being Nottingham's equivalent of the high-density housing so popular in the East End of London where Mr Rackman and an associate by the name of Dunnett rented property. (Forget this socialist sixth form crap, McVay, you're part of the rat race and earning damn good money now lad).

The Meadows where the locals all recall radio's Two Way Family Favourites and Cliff Michelmore receiving a letter from Crocus Street. How lovely the name sounded, said Cliff, evoking memories of green fields, flowers growing by hedgerows and sparrows chirping in cloudless skies. Whereas in fact the only sounds heard in Crocus Street, The Meadows, were communal lavatories being flushed in the cobbled back yards that separated ten or twelve houses in this desperate slum area where everyone was poor but happy.

Steak...Diana Ross

I've heard this story more than once . . . this morning
I've heard it again just before Billy drops off his eggs and
earns himself a fiver from the local fruit and veg man in his
village of Ruddington. Meadow Lane at last - not certain
what was going to kill me first, Billy's eternal reminiscing
about the good old days and good old boys and the good
old, long-lost characters, or the overwhelming aroma of
spearmint he's chewing machine-gun fashion to conceal
the stale smell of last night's ale consumption.

The session is light. The gaffer is pleased. His fellow
Jock manager across the Trent, Allan Brown, is livid we
got a draw. Jimmy's out-thought and out-manoeuvred the
bastard in tactics. Nothing like nobbling a fellow Scot. "A
quick chuke up round the track eh, Jackson," he tells Jack
Wheeler. "These boys are ready for the battle, eh."
Jimmy's in his regulation brown suit, dark blue shirt with
green check and blue Notts County tie.

Suddenly I feel sick.

This isn't hard track work, just a gentle jog then some
alleged sprints and a few 'half laps'.

"Come on you bloody man, Brian. Stubbsy, you can do
better than that" - signs of panic as Jack struggles to keep
the pros, young and old, in check. We respect him but like
the schoolkids most of us are, if we can cheat on
homework or in class, we will.

Stubbo, unwell from inhaling 20 Woodbine and
partaking of several gallons of Shipstones, the local brew
known as the Black Death, the night before, feigns injury
and limps back to the treatment room for a fag. The first
team squad are about done when Jimmy emerges down
the tunnel and on to the playing surface.

He's changed into full training gear. Whistle on elbow attached by string, he takes a training ball and marches up to the penalty area in front of the Spion Kop, empty terraces and the half-time scoreboard awaiting his arrival.

By now we're jogging down the halfway line towards his goal, unguarded by goalkeeper or nets. Jimmy places the ball on the penalty spot and takes three deliberate steps back. He looks around at the terraces. A short pause, as we run behind his goal.

A quick 'peep' on the whistle and he waltzes up, swaggering his hips and smacks the ball low to the right, hitting the stanchion at the back of the goal. His right arm punches the air and he looks for approval as we walk away for a bath.

"He wasn't going to stop that one boss," big Braddy beams mockingly.

"Not a bit of it Wesley, son. That was the perfect penalty son, you mark my fucking words, Bomber (Braddy's nickname for plundering goals in the air, I expect)."

Jimmy gathers up the ball and puts it down on the spot again. Pregnant pause. 'Peep' - pick that fucker out you little beauty.

His manic Glaswegian laugh follows us down the tunnel. No characters left at all, Billy.

Saturday, March 9

I'm Free, de-de-de, de-de-de-de-de, I'm Free, And I'm waiting for you to follow me. I call upon Roger Daltrey

to put my case today, m'lud. That is, no McKenzie in the Sheffield Wednesday side. Back to the creativity of midfield. They can bloody well track my forward runs, not I their every bowel movement.

Well that's the plan, anyway. Eric McManus has other ideas, though. Eric the Ever Ready, our Emerald hero last Sunday, Irish clot after half an hour.

No danger as he drops a header from Mike Prendergast behind his line. 1-0. The back four have only two to bloody well mark today but they might as well be 22.

Brian Joicey makes it two from nothing and big Prendergast adds a third. Super Bloody Mac, Stubbs and Needham join missing persons list. Half time: No-one talks. Let's get out and put it right. Needham heads wide, Masson volleys one in which Peter Springett tips over.

But why is Brindley's aim so ragged this afternoon? The silence of his right boot flailing through the Meadow Lane inner stratosphere is eerie. Normally there's the thud of sharpened metal stud on weak and unwilling outside left ankle or shin flesh followed by the pig-like squeal of said recipient of Billy's calling card. Occasionally they reach their intended destination, Block A, Row B, Main Stand with or without the assistance of the St John's Ambulance stretcher.

Today, though, Brindley is taking prisoners. "Give him a fucking reminder Billy," Masson urges as another busy bee disguised in Wednesday's yellow and blue away strip ambles by him down the left flank. "What's the fucking matter with you today."

"A touch too much bubbly at the Playboy, skipper?" if only he had the breath to draw would have probably been

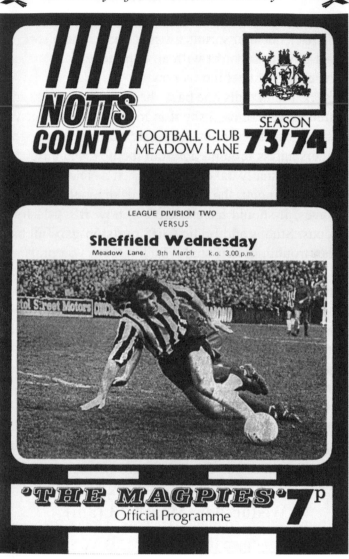

Without the menace of Duncan McKenzie to concern us, I am released from my shadow-marking and allowed a more flexible midfield role. The creative talents flow freely - we lose 5-1.

19

Billy's reply through grinding teeth as he picks himself up off his backside and sprints away to make some sort (any sort) of physical contact with an opponent.

The crowd are behind us now.

Archie Mann pulls one back then I found myself going by three players only to shoot in to the side netting. Why the fuck can't I shoot straight? Bradd beats three defenders and is brought down in the box. Penalty.

Masson usually takes them but it's The Claw who steps up. Springett, the little bastard, dives the right way and saves. It should have been 3-2, now it's 4-1. Joicey drifts past Stubbs and Eddie Cliff, our stop-gap full back, without troubling their studs. Tackle them you prats. Just one tackle. Remember last Sunday. They shall not pass. His shot slips under Eric's body. We are doomed.

A minute later a midget named Eric Potts beats what passes for our offside trap and it's five. Blow that bloody whistle, ref.

Suddenly I've put on weight again.

Sunday, March 10

5-1 at home. Jesus. Watched Monty Python later. Not quite as absurd as our display yesterday.

Wednesday, March 13 (am)

There's nothing like a relaxing five-a-side and a bit of fun and games to boost team morale. That and a right good thrash at a few pubs and clubs to break up the week. The main objective for the five-a-side on the ash and

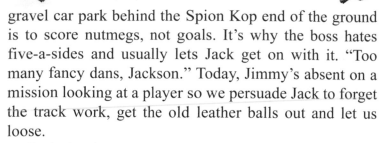

gravel car park behind the Spion Kop end of the ground
is to score nutmegs, not goals. It's why the boss hates
five-a-sides and usually lets Jack get on with it. "Too
many fancy dans, Jackson." Today, Jimmy's absent on a
mission looking at a player so we persuade Jack to forget
the track work, get the old leather balls out and let us
loose.

Such is the excitement that we lose a couple of
footballs en route to the car park. Two apprentices balloon
them over the wall that separates the ground from the
back-to-back Meadows housing that is still standing -
only just. Very soon, it's all going in the Corporation's
slum clearance programme.

For now, though, it's best not to ask for our ball back
mister. A few of the residents are Forest fans.

The five-a-side (actually it's more eight apiece with
the apprentices and Jack playing in goal). Dear old Jack.
He's going on 60 and still stands in goal when we're short
in training. Won't duck or dive from the most lethal drive
Stubbo or Bernie can muster. Those two have just about
the hardest shot from a dead ball in the club although put
it on Stubbo's head and the ball travels faster and further.
A bit like his control.

"You bloody man, Bernie," Jack says, parrying another
piledriver from between the five-a-side nets. Tears,
tantrums and nutmegs in abundance. The general rule is
to avoid Masson. If he's in one of his moods (knows the
face but blanks you in a manner that suggests you are less
than amoeba level in the scheme of things) he uses his far
superior skills to demean what shred of talent you
imagined you possessed. There isn't a hole deep enough

to hide inside. The Nottingham Pork Butchers' League, Division Eight is the next career move.

Result, 18-13 to Masson's lot, 23 nutmegs although ten of those were on apprentices and Jack which don't count.

Back in the dressing room, there is but one topic of debate.

"Who gets the Gellow Bib, then?" Pedro Richards, a young full back on the verge of the first team asks the question fearing it could be him. Born in London, reared in a remote northern Spanish village until he was 12 then brought by his mum to live in The Meadows, he hasn't quite mastered the Queen's English yet. The difference between swimming and women, at least in pronunciation, are other glaring gaps in his English comprehension as well as an unfortunate habit of calling a well known Scottish comedian with a penchant for dressing in women's clothing Stanley Bastard.

"So, the Gellow Bib, Jack. Who is it, you bruddy man?" The 'Gellow Bib' is reserved for the worst five-a-side performance and though a bit of jovial banter, nobody actually wants to possess the taboo talisman for a week.

Masson is out of the question. Far too good, far too bloody miserable and moody. There is but one choice. Happy Eric Probert, at £35,000 our record signing from Burnley last year.

He accepts it with all the good grace a Yorkshireman can muster in times of adversity, launching a hot cup of mash man Albert's tea at the door just above Pedro's head before storming off into the bath in mock rage. Oblivious, Pedro etches the name PROBERT on the yellow bib in black Magic Marker. "He's only yellous," he laughs and we all try hard to get the yoke.

Wednesday March 13 (pm)

The troops are gathered for more morale boosting. Watching the reserves toil in the bitter mid-March night air from the near empty Main Stand lifts most of the first teamers. The significance is not lost on Bradd and Brindley. They're down in the Centenary Room having decided another pint of Home Ales Five Star will lift their spirits rather better than 45 minutes of a North Midlands League game. Who am I to argue?

The ghosts of Wednesday past, Potts, Joicey and Poltergeist who eluded our back four as if invisible, have long been exorcised. For this is Wednesday present and the night is young. The last occasion players can officially be seen to be throwing alcohol down their necks and still avoid the wrath of Joe Public.

Jack Wheeler's words of wisdom are being drowned by Suzi Quatro on the jukebox of the Newcastle Arms.

"If you're out in the week, David," I could still recall Jack's sobering and thoughtful words above the lyrics of Devil Gate Drive and the thought of so much flabby flesh crammed inside so little leather.

"Always hold a half pint glass in your hand instead of a pint. It doesn't matter if it's orange and lemonade in the pint glass, the punters will still think you're drinking pints of beer on a Wednesday night."

In respect to Jack, I have just a half pint glass. One in each hand, that is. I am so clever.

Steak...Diana Ross

At the 99 Club, overlooking the river on Trent Bridge, Forest and County players gather to discuss tactics. A pincer movement on a gaggle of women led by the formidable Grace (amazing to her many friends and admirers) is considered the way forward. It's all a game, of course. It's the same girls, the same blokes and usually the same time and place.

Disillusioned, dismayed and drunk.

2am: Alone and unloved in the council house at Clifton. A gin and tonic for company and my old mate Nick Drake on the record player, the man who makes Leonard Cohen sound like The Carpenters.

"Time has told me, not to ask for more . . .". But it's all right. It's safe to listen to Five Leaves Left if you're on the ground floor sat well away from sharpened objects.

Thursday March 14

The boss is away in London today, signing, we think, a new player before transfer deadline. Ronnie Fenton takes training. An unpleasant Geordie, he has no discernible redeeming features. He talks through clenched teeth, genuinely in pain if he has to smile and false if he breaks into laughter. On reflection, perhaps he has a redeeming feature, well a feature at any rate. A dick almost as long and wide as the Bomber's but since the pair seldom share the same bath, it has been a matter of conjecture as to who has the biggest. A ruler to measure the two or standing side by side has been suggested. It is an unlikely prospect. There is only one big prick in the club, anyway.

24

Objectionable as a deputy, he is unsufferable when in charge but true to form he lays on a fun session to impress. A sly jibe at the gaffer dropped in pointedly, shrewdly almost, enhances his popularity with the apprentices and younger pros, most of whom he has played with in the reserves and coaxed in the youth team. But he must beware the spy in the camp, wee Masson, Jimmy's "jewel in the crown, Jesus Christ" as he once told the television in a rare interview. Masson can bend the gaffer's ear and is the only one who can get his undivided attention - and Ronnie knows it. He is such a manipulative git, but I suppose you need to be a devious sod to survive in this game. A good session, though, mainly because Thursday is sweat day, the last real chance to cleanse the body before the weekend.

Play hard, work hard is the doctrine by which the likes of Brindley, Stubbo and Braddy survive. The curfew for drinking is Wednesday - normally the day of rest before the night on the town. A general meeting up then the thrill of the chase that involves being shunted around several clubs early in the morning in pursuit of something different. The prerequisite is that several gallons of beer then spirits must be consumed in the process. It perhaps heightens the thrill or maybe just deadens the sensations because inevitably it is back to the 99 Club and the happy hunting ground. In between you might be lucky enough to get a lift in the Braddmobile - a yellow and black Ford Cortina 2000XL, fluffy dice inclusive. Then that's it until Saturday, 5.05pm and around the country, from Boothferry Park to Home Park (two very nice players' bars), the festivities begin again. At Meadow Lane, first out of the big bath, an aroma of sanitised carbolic in his trail, goes Probey followed by the hardcore. Thereafter, a fortnight's drinking for the average bloke is crammed joyously into the available and permitted days.

Come Wednesday night it is as though a magic wand is waved. The thought occurs of a Cinderella in reverse; the pumpkins revert to glistening chariots and thoroughbred horses. Well not quite. But after a Thursday morning game, the purgatory of a few doggies (short sprints up and down a marked area) back at the track and a bloody good sweat and it is as if nothing has happened, not a drop of alcohol has passed the lips all week.

Except the whiff of stale beer on Probey's breath betrays him, this despite five Wrigley's chewed enthusiastically from the moment he walks into the ground (morning Eric; mmm) to the moment he leaves (bye Eric; mmm).

There is also the state of his kit after training, dripping wet with the stench of Tetley's best bitter hanging in the air nearby. A personal aroma for the £35,000 man.

Actually he has cheered up by noon, mainly because the little man hammering inside his cranium to get out has probably gone for lunch and knocked off for the day.

"Quiet night last night, Probey?" Brindley quips but his victim will not be drawn. He is in and out of the bath in record time, even for him. You never know with Probey whether or not he is going to break the curfew. The quiet ones are the worst, without doubt.

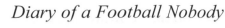
Friday, March 15

The Squirrel returns with Ray O'Brien, £15,000 from Manchester United and an Eire international. A full back with a nice touch, good left foot and an Irish accent that is impossible to understand. His arrival means Bob Worthington is on his way. Bob, who came from Middlesbrough with Masson, one of the gaffer's first signings who has served the club and Jimmy so well. Six foot tall, a thumping shot on him and a great sense of humour. He was a stalwart of the teams that gained promotion from the Fourth to the Second but the crowd has been getting on his back. As well as Jimmy, now and again. "He's got one trick, one fucking trick. Watch, he opens the legs and the ball is on its way." This was Jimmy's pre-match talk against Forest last Boxing Day talking about McKenzie. Thirty seconds into the match there is a long ball played into McKenzie's feet, along the floor with pace. The Forest way, of course. Bob prepares to launch McKenzie into Row B of the Main Stand, just over the dugout where Jimmy and Jack are sitting. A premeditated run-up of about 20 yards and then suddenly, legs open, ball and McKenzie are gone down the line and somehow Ian Bowyer puts a header over the bar into the old Meadow Lane stand from his cross. In the meantime Bob has slid off the pitch, landing virtually at the home dugout. "Jesus fucking Christ …" you can hear Jimmy starting to rebuke Bob for not heeding his warning but the rest is drowned by the noise of the capacity crowd. There is no sentiment in this game. "It was always so McVay," Brindley would point out ad infinitum on his egg round.

"It will always be so." Bob knows it is time to move and Brindley knows it is likely to be his turn next. Sooner rather than later, with Pedro being touted as the next right back.

He tells the story of his Easter a few years ago. "The ankle was out here," he has explained once, twice or maybe a dozen times over the season, putting aside his pint of beer and gesturing his hands to imitate the size and shape of a football. "I got done on the Saturday and we were playing Brentford, eleven in the morning kick off on the Monday. There was no chance. 'But boss (there is a hint of mockery in the voice here), but boss I cannae play.'

"Away with you Billy. Jackson! Jackson! They don't know what a bad ankle is. Jesus, when you can't get the bellbottom trousers on because it's the size of a fucking beach ball, that's a bad ankle."

And of course Jack, tenderly, gingerly then sharply prodding Billy's ankle to release the congealed bad blood and get some of the bruising out, would agree without a hint of falsehood. "Yes boss."

"So Jack strapped me up with sticky tape and plaster and I played in bloody agony," Billy has whet his whistle and is in full flow now. "And the best of it was that little rat Masson. Gave me a bollocking for making a mistake that cost us a goal. And he knew the score. But when he wanted looking after if he was getting a bit of bother from someone. 'Next time he comes your way, Billy, sort him out.' The little shithouse."

Of course, Billy was only too happy to oblige. "Cleanly, Macca. I always took the ball first," he insisted even if the evidence on Saturday afternoons and in training suggested otherwise. And so to Bob, who having done his time, will now be sacrificed back to the levels from which he aspired. The end of an era, to be sure. And the worst of it is, at any rate for quite a few women I know, it will probably be the end of those infrequent visits from Frank, in his Elvis boots and cowboy hat, swaggering around Meadow Lane to see his brother play.

Saturday, March 16

All roads lead to Huddersfield and the George Hotel for a pre-match meal. They must have slaughtered a herd of Aberdeen's best cattle by the amount of charred meat that is served up before us. Geoff, the bus driver, is behind schedule. His ear lobes turn a deep crimson as Jimmy chirps away at him. It's not Geoff's fault, of course, but he takes it on the chin. A smashing bloke, Geoff. During the war he served on U-boats and if he had his way, I know who he might have closed the hatch on as the submarine plummeted to the ocean depths. Even though we are half an hour late, the steak is paid for and we must consume it - quickly.

In the restaurant, a hushed silence falls over the squad. Brindley has rallied the troops to observe feeding time at the zoo.

"Aye, have you any red sauce, lassie?" Jimmy asks the waitress at a secluded table in the corner.

She duly fetches it, the players watching her every movement, awaiting the ritual finale to this regular theatre. A push and a shake and Heinz tomato ketchup

lands in abundance next to Jimmy's medium rare. It is then, and only then, that Jimmy repeats a scene witnessed in hundreds of eateries up and down the country as he licks the bottle's neck clean of its sauce before replacing the top. The young girl is horrified; Brindley and Co are having convulsions. No matter how many times you see it, there is always that element of the unknown. Will he or won't he? But then he always does.

At Deepdale, despite the carnivorous appetite we cruise to a 2-0 win. I am restored to a defensive back five. "Don't play football son," Jimmy tells Bernie, one of our central three. "Give it to David if you're in trouble." Praise indeed from the gaffer. What's he after?

Tuesday, March 19

Training on the track before day off tomorrow. Six laps, six horseshoes and then six half laps. 666, the boss is trying to tell us something. David Needham and Jon Nixon sail through it, natural athletes, pedigree material. Stubbo and Brindley - more like pedigree chum.

Albert, the master tea brewer delivers another pot of a steaming hot brew to the home team dressing room. Albert reckons he once boxed against Bendigo, Nottingham's own bare knuckled pugilist and champion of the world, or so Albert says at any rate. The public house named after him in Sneinton is as near as he ever got to the great man. Just for laughs, a pair of socks is dropped into the stew. They are Brindley's and he is not a happy bunny. Probert gets the blame and all hell breaks loose but they kiss and make up after Brindley pours the tea over PJ Probey's wedding tackle.

Honours even. In the corner, Masson sits and deliberates and shakes his head. All week he has reported for training without so much as a 'good morning' to anyone. Now he is on his way home without a good bye. Miserable bastard.

DON MASSON:

The man who would light up a football pitch during 90 minutes with his considerable talent, Masson could darken a dressing room in seconds with one sullen look. Master of the weighted pass and weighty expression.

## Friday, March 22

Visit Susan (sister) in hospital and her first baby, Natalie Jane. 7lb 7oz. Time for me to move on from home. Too many late nights and early mornings chewing the fat with nobody in particular and getting nowhere fast. I really envy some of the lads who come back from college and university for holidays. I hate bloody students but it's not a bad old life on campus. Should I finish and apply as a mature student? £25 per week and forty quid a point persuades me otherwise.

I didn't think I could get more than 80 out of this Fiat but it's surprising how fast it can go when escaping Chesterfield on a dank Friday night after watching our reserves get beat in the North Midlands League Cup.

It's also amazing how fast those bloody Range Rovers with blue flashing lights on top can travel on the M1. "Sorry officer, I forgot about the fuel shortage and the 50mph speed limit," I said. "Name?" "Dave McVay." "Don't you play for Notts County?" he asked. "Well yes, I'm afraid so," I replied, flattered and rather impressed by his recognition faculties. "You're nicked!" Any relation to the Scottish Massons, I refrained from asking.

Sunday, March 24 (morning reflection)

The Flying Horse Hotel is a wonderful establishment. Seven bars inside one of Nottingham's oldest and most graceful buildings, set in the shadow of the

Council House, a testament to unchecked civic pomposity and pretension. (Enough of the 6th form lefty McVay).

Apart from money, your best bet of gaining attention or reputation in the old Horse is to be trendy, bendy or a professional footballer; that is, you shop at Paul Smith or the Birdcage boutiques, you are queer or you play for Forest or County. Normally the clientele of the Flyer manage two out of those three. It is a vibrant focal point, bloody expensive but a place to be seen and noticed nonetheless.

Unfortunately I was a little bit too noticed to one drunken yob last night who climbed over the railings at the pub's entrance under radar level and landed a right hander smack on the lip - blood everywhere. Police patrolling the Market Square broke up the scrimmage that followed with my drinking companions, getting a little mixed up as to their role as the cavalry sounding the retreat at the first hint of bother.

"I'll never pull with this bruiser now," I told a young constable attempting to avoid recrimination. "You wouldn't without it mate," and I was on my way for a few soothing pints of lager in the bar that never closes at the Trent Bridge Inn. Shane O'Neill, Martin's younger brother, vehement, volatile and passionate about Irish politics as ever but it eases the recovery. Almost forgot, beat West Bromwich Albion 1-0 in the afternoon. 7 out of 10 in The People this morning. Memo: Must buy John Ross (reporter) whisky after the game. Surely my turn for the Sheriff's Badge (star man in the People) soon.

Tuesday, March 26

David Smith, aka Smudger or Smithy, an apprentice with most likely the filthiest mind and habits of any human being on God's earth, has further revelations from the diary of J Sirrel. One of his duties is to sweep up and clean the gaffer's office but he sneaks a peak at JS's personal notes while Pedro, whose grasp of written English is on a par with his attempts at the spoken word, stands lookout at the door. "You'll never guess what," Smudger teases the senior players who all have a vested interest in transfer talk. Needham, Stubbs and even Masson show an interest. He would. Miserable he may be but he is destined for the first division. We know it and so does he.

Smudger treads a fine line. If he takes it too far, he'll get a good hiding or at the very least his balls blacked with boot polish. "Nothing to report except Nixo, there was something about Peterborough United making an inquiry." That will suffice for now.

Wednesday, March 27

Day off. Golf with Smudger, the Bolt and Vint. The Bolt plays his golf like his football. A million miles an hour, a ferocious long ball off the tee and not an ounce of finesse around the green. He wins easily.

Thursday, March 28

Eric McManus stood in for Nixo to help with some coaching at Greenholme, a private prep school on Derby Road. Five pounds for two afternoons a week, taking a bunch of spoilt little brats to Harvey Hadden Stadium before throwing a ball in the middle and letting the unruly sods get on with it. There are perks. Mrs Breem, the headmistress, an eccentric sort who runs the school with a rod of iron. And then the mothers picking up at 3.15. "Eric, look at the state of that will you," as an impeccably groomed, classy lady squeezed out of her Mercedes Sports to gather Benjamin or James or Giles or whoever.

"Fuppin' nice car, McVay." Poor Eric. He was counting his money and he needed to. Young children, mortgage and a wife with extravagant tastes and still he can't afford a decent pair of shoes. No wonder he's playing out of his skin to keep on the first team bonus. And of course replacing the more senior coach he was paid £7.50 for his two days a week. He rolled back in neutral with the engine of his dirty old Cortina turned off for the first part of a three point turn. "Saves the petrol, boy" Eric explains. Hard to tell if he was joking.

Friday, March 29

Up late last night listening to One Live Badger and The Yes Album. Your Move must be the best LP track of all time. Well it's an opinion. Arranged to see Nixo at Broad Marsh bus station before a 'chuke up' at Meadow

Lane. He was standing near the newsagents, in between two racks of magazines and looking more than a little furtive. Glancing over his shoulder, he was reading some dubious material - pictures of men and women (I think) in gas masks, leather suits and all manner of apparatus, and generally wrapped up as tight as a tin of John West sardines. Just then, a young, angelic girl approaches. "Excuse me, Mr Nixon, but could I have your autograph?" she asked with her proud and beaming mother in silent vigil no more than 10 yards away. "Certainly dear," Nixo said, turning a brilliant shade of purple. He rested her autograph book on Gas Mask Gertie and her rubber friends and duly obliged with his signature. "Off you go now," he hurried her away before her mum, clearly a big fan of our flying winger, can come any closer. Jon, a former schoolteacher and a very funny man, but what would his pupils, and his wife, think of him now. I couldn't stifle a manic fit of giggles from the other side of the rack. The Daily Mirror and the Express travel with him to London for stimulation. Gas Mask Weekly remains back at the newsagent's.

Saturday, March 30

0-0 at Cold Blow Lane against Millwall. Can Saturday afternoons get any worse?

Thursday, April 4

Finally moved out of home. Bingham, the village of the damned and remarkably few different surnames, awaits for me and Geoff Collier.

Friday, April 5

We had tried to keep our relationship a secret but it was to no avail. "Here come the odd couple," Nixo ventured sarcastically as we walked into training, not hand in hand mind you, after our first night spent together in the semi-detached love nest at Bingham.

Odd? Possibly. Collier is a veteran of non-league football, goals galore for Macclesfield Town on the Northern Premier League circuit and pussy galore at a variety of northern nightclubs from Manchester to Blackpool. At 23, he has come late into the full-time game and on both counts of goals and pussy, I am the novice. "Don't you two go falling out over the washing-up."

MEMO: Must sort out the TV and licence, iron and ironing board, hoover and milk round. Bloody obvious who wears the trousers in our house.

Saturday, April 6

It could have been us but of course it wasn't to be. Away today, via Bawtry's Crown Hotel and 'red sauce lassie' to Middlesbrough, champions of the Second Division. Jack Charlton leads them out as manager for

one of their last chances to be fêted by the crowd at Ayresome Park this season. The contrast couldn't be starker with my first game of the season, a debut at Selhurst Park when Malcolm Allison swaggered out to crush the carrot-crunching upstarts from Oop North and just up from the Third Division. Nicknames for his players on the tracksuits, too - the Shuffler, the Joker, Charlie Cooke, Don Rogers, Derek Possee with the champagne already on ice. Never has a 4-1 victory in London tasted so sweet and an £80 bonus on top of 25 quid in my pay packet. Untaxed!! This football lark is easy. "Enjoy the day son," Jimmy had slapped my thigh in the dugout later. "It might never come again." Jimmy was full of restraining philosophy. "Good morning boss." "Not so good if yer six feet under, eh, David." "No boss."

Now it was nearing the end of a long, hard nine months. Crystal Palace were near the bottom, another relegation loomed. Middlesbrough, no nicknames, no frills but plenty of grit and a few players who could play a bit! Alan Foggon, Stuart Boam, McMordie, Maddren. They were top and not by fluke.

For 45 minutes it really could have been us. 0-0 at half time, no problems. Then the Bolt decides to have a brainwave. He doesn't get many but when he does, the fallout is frightening. 1-0 becomes 2-0 when Neddy puts one in his own net. Now Boro are showing why they are champions. Wor Jack must have thrown a few cups during the interval. Stubbs, Needham totally out of it. We all are. Wherever you cover, there is an extra red-shirted player. Whenever you try to counter, there is an extra

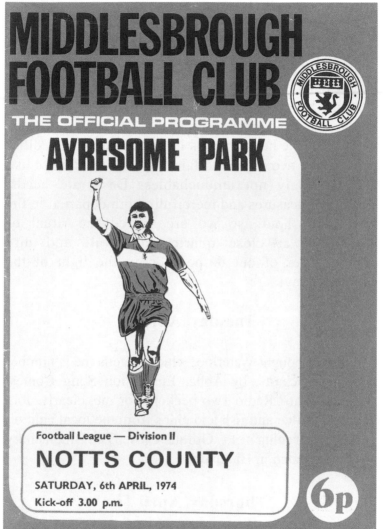

MIDDLESBROUGH FOOTBALL CLUB

THE OFFICIAL PROGRAMME

AYRESOME PARK

Football League — Division II

NOTTS COUNTY

SATURDAY, 6th APRIL, 1974
Kick-off 3.00 p.m.

6p

With six games remaining, Jack Charlton's Middlesbrough have
secured the Second Division Championship. Despite our side's
natural inclination to party, we are unable to celebrate after a
serious 4-0 defeat.

man. That is a team full of confidence. You feel as if you are taking on fifteen men and you know at least five of your own are below par on the day. The self-belief in your own ability is being sucked out at a rate of knots. The bubble burst, we sink like a lead balloon. 4-0 at the death, it could have been fourteen. The ghosts of Sheffield Wednesday have returned.

At least the house breaks its duck that night. Collier brings back two of the old faithful, unfaithful more like and definitely not untouchables. Desperate needs, desperate measures and mercifully both departed in the wee small hours so we are spared the ritual of witnessing at close quarters the full and dire consequences of our desperation in the light of the following day!

Tuesday, April 9

Collier has bought Waterloo, which he tells me is number one in the charts, by Abba, Eurovision Song Contest winners. Who? Radio Two beckons for me, clearly. Joni Mitchell's Blue and fish and chips from the local chip oil passes the evening at 17, Gillotts Close. The Bloomsbury Set reincarnated in Bingham.

Thursday, April 11

There comes a time in the rites of passage of every young man when he must urinate in a friend's wardrobe. And so it came to pass last night following a cricket club dance at the Wagon and Horses, a charming

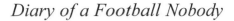

pub, well it was until I arrived, owned by Bill Whare, the former Forest full back who won the FA Cup with them back in 1959. An acrimonious evening with too much to drink and say before driving back with John Watson and slept on the bedroom floor of his parents' house at Silverdale, the Wimpey Estate across the border from Clifton where the posh folk reside. Mr and Mrs Watson ring today. They are not amused. Somehow, gawd knows how, I've even added a cascading fountain effect in three of the four side drawers. There's real talent. Extremely angry of Silverdale they are. "I'll pay for the dry cleaning myself," I offered weakly. "Goodbye David." There is a chilling finality to it all. Were they never young and in charge of a wayward penis once? Felt bloody rough all day and looked it but scored two in training against the reserves in Jimmy's 900th practice match. Knowing my movements the night before, Collier was mightily impressed by my powers of recovery. So was I.

Friday, April 12

The Newark Advertiser rang. Yes, the Newark Advertiser. They want to do a feature on Collier and me living at Bingham. "You will have to dust and hoover for that," Brindley, planning a summer of cricket behind the stumps and egg delivery, pipes up.

Grandad said ask for a fiver - he wants 5%. I do miss them all at home - after 12 years in the same place. Depression sets in, alone at night thinking about them. Collier gone home for a weekend of debauchery. Lucky

bastard. Pre-season to start on July 10 goes up on the notice board. Haven't even finished this one yet.

P.S. Another grovelling apology to the Watsons to no avail.

Saturday, April 13

Notts County v Bolton Wanderers at the Lane - Land of the Giants meets Godzilla, King Kong and friends. Step forward Sam Allardyce and Stubbo, rivals for the title of the game's most glamorous centre backs. Both are kind to No.9s and want to work with animals when they retire. They strive for world peace.

Peter Thompson, formerly of Liverpool and England and the man dropped by Alf Ramsay to make way for his wingless wonders, nutmegs me twice from 10 yards; same routine, same place, defending in the bottom left hand corner of the pitch. Write a thousand times: Must Keep Legs Shut When Old England Lag Approaches; Must Keep Legs Shut When Old England Lag Approaches; Must Keep . . . . It ends 0-0 and early for me, substituted with 20 minutes left. When the number is being pulled out of the pack by Jack, it's normally me, the Bolt or Vinter who react like Pavlov's dogs and head for the dugout. Today it was I who gets the nod.

Can't come to terms with this wide role on the right side of midfield. Yearn to be back marking McKenzie or in the back four. "Stick at it son," Jack tells me. "Better to be playing out of position in the first team than where you want in the reserves." Jack, you bloody man, you always have an answer. Invariably it's right but it's only prevarication on my part.

Escorted an unknown quantity back to Bingham but couldn't raise a smile. "Confessions of an impotent teenager". Scoreless at Bingham. So it can get worse of a weekend than a goalless draw at Millwall.

'Notts start a new era with McVay' was the headline in the local sports paper tonight.

Monday, April 15

Dropped versus Cardiff City. Good. Notts start a new era without McVay, perhaps they meant to say. They will miss me. But of course they don't, even if it all ends 1-1. They say it's a team game but if you are not in the team, it quickly becomes every man - and in terms of the players' wives every woman - for themselves. Team spirit? It is an act of self-delusion if you really believe you are willing the likes of Probey, who has replaced me, and the others on. Some are worse, little Smudger who applauds a good move down the right then curses Masson under his breath. In the far section of the old wooden Main Stand (built in 1911), the rejects sit po-faced, hoping for a disaster to befall individuals and the team in their absence. Close by are the players' wives, a breed apart whose vicarious existence means they must endure the terrace taunts and acid criticism first hand that their husbands seldom hear.

Margaret Masson, a lovely lady, full of life and fun; what is that about opposites attracting? Just behind her, a charmless individual is calling for the head of Masson. The abuse is personal but Mrs M, pretty dignified and perhaps hardened to it all now, remains calm. They all do today but it is not always so. How can it be when the person sitting one row behind is demanding that your better half is crap and he should be sacked forthwith by management. The only wage earner emasculated in the household and, in the case of Sandra Mann or Cath Brindley, two or three bairns to feed.

For the younger set, wives and girlfriends, there is perhaps even more to lose. A vicarious existence maybe but they wallow in the reflected glory and who would deny them that.

Now it is the turn of Probey to be the target of abuse. The Yorkshire terrier has lost his bite and perception. The drink is slowing him down. A wee bit tubby at times, he carries weight badly but he is the salt of the earth - nothing is too much trouble for Probey and despite the fact I was dropped to make way for him, enough is enough.

Every professional footballer has empathy with a fellow pro when the crowd begins to slaughter him. The terraces sniff a wounded animal and close in for the kill and on the pitch, suddenly your legs are made of lead and you are treading water. Running as in the dream sequence, standing on the spot, almost getting there in slow motion only to be denied at the last moment.

Some swim, many sink and every player has been there. Well mostly every player except the likes of Steve Carter, Flash Carter, Get Carter, the little winger from Manchester City who beats full backs just for fun - then just for good measure goes back and gives them another chance. Sporting like that in Great Yarmouth, where he was born.

"For fuck's sake Flash, get one over," Braddy has been known to plead during the course of the game. The timing of his run has been perfect and there are few better headers of the ball in the game. As a centre forward he thrives on the delivery of the ball from the byline but Flash has other ideas. A quick crowd-pleasing jaunt that fades into nothing before disappearing up his own backside. And on the penalty spot, Bradd is exasperated. Jimmy, in the dugout, is no happier.

"The little c***" and he means it.

Flash Carter because of the fashion sense he learned from the high-fliers of Maine Road; Get Carter because if Bradd ever gets hold of him, his prancing days on the right wing are over.

Probey has sunk without trace. He can probably smell the froth on the pint of best bitter which is guiding him to the Centenary Bar via the Main Stand dressing room. Today he is subbed by Flash. How that must hurt. The lads scrape a draw. There is a gaunt expression in Probey's face in the Centenary Bar later. The season is nearing an end but for some in our ranks, it is already over. Magaluf and Benidorm beckon. The wives insist on it.

Wednesday, April 17

Reporter from the Newark Advertiser arrives with photographer. Insists on a picture of the happy couple outside chez nous at the front gates. Help.

Steak...Diana Ross

Advertiser, April 20, 1974—Page 11

McVAY AND COLLIER TEAM-UP AT BINGHAM

IN A season of Second Division consolidation, one of the successes among the Notts County playing staff has been David McVay (19), who was playing schoolboy football a year ago.

David has recently rented a house with Reserve striker Geoff Collier in Bingham, and this week he told the Advertiser about his rise into soccer's big-league.

He was captain of the Fairham Comprehensive School side that won the English Schools Individual Trophy last year and during the close season he signed full professional forms with Notts County — after only three reserve games.

"I was surprised by how quickly I got into the first team," he said, "but once I had strung several games together near Christmas I began to feel more at ease. I don't think I'm quite Second Division material yet, but when you are young effort and enthusiasm make up for lack of experience."

Although David is modest about his ability, County manager Jimmy Sirrel has sufficient confidence in him to play David in mid-field and defence.

"At first I didn't like the centre-back role because of the responsibility," said David. "I played my first game in mid-field at Sunderland where we won 2-1 and I was quite pleased with my performance. However, after several games in the middle I am now back in defence and enjoying my role."

Teacher

David's immediate ambi

Carlisle a favour today when County go to London to face Orient and he thinks the Magpies have every chance of improving their impressive away record.

"Our home and away records are now identical," he pointed out, "but I think our home form could have been improved with better support from the crowd.

"The three-up, three-down system has provoked criticism in recent weeks and it is said that more clubs are playing defensively, but David supported the League's initiative: "The Second Division is probably the best example of the new idea as things are so tight. I think it has encouraged teams to play more attractively on opponents grounds, for instance Sheffield Wednesday came to Meadow lane and went forward throughout the match."

Prolific

Life has certainly changed over the last nine months for David McVay, but this level-headed youngster plans to take things step by step and, under the careful guidance of manager Jimmy Sirrel, he looks to have a bright future with Notts County.

For Geoff Collier the season has been one of frustration in a year that promised so much. He had been playing non-league soccer with Macclesfield

Relaxing at their new home in Bingham, Notts County footballers David McVay (left) and Geoff Collier look forward to mounting a Second Division promotion challenge with the Magpies next season.

Cherubina qualifies

Exciting sailing

Thursday, April 18

Greenholme School 3, Dagfa House 1. My first victory as a coach although having experienced a coaching session with Howard Wilkinson in my younger days, life is far too short to start getting mixed up with the Lilleshall set. Even Pedro has refused to go on a training session with the England Youth set up. They are not his cup of tea and it is easy to see why. "Too many arse lickers." He is a better prospect at right back than Viv [Anderson] across the Trent with Forest but that attitude will not endear him to the England fraternity and the arses they aspire to lick.

46

Still, guiding Greenholme to a win must be a considerable feather in my cap. Girls not screaming and boys being co-operative. It was all a rather pleasant experience, not a chore at all. One of the young lads cut his knee but 'mummy' insisted that he stayed on the pitch. Stupid bitch! Made final arrangements for party at house on Saturday. Will be returning from London having been picked for first team away to Orient. Saturday.

Friday, April 19

Travelled to South Mimms Post House for overnight stay. It is not the first time that my sartorial elegance at the dinner table has been remarked upon. Jack was once told by Jimmy to remove me from the table because the t-shirt I was wearing was an embarrassment, particularly as the Hartlepool squad sitting next door to us was immaculately turned out - at least in the eyes of the gaffer. Well he does like his fluorescent shirts, a bit of colour and width in his matching kipper ties and those wonderful oval collars. I've relented but still prefer a pair of cords and a loose shirt minus tie which naturally is an object of ridicule to the likes of Brindley and Bradd. Any comments, they know, will infuriate and wind the boss up. But they are not in the mood tonight and the meal passes quietly.

Saturday, April 20

Masson in fine form at Leyton Stadium. Talking, encouraging, just fucking inspirational really. But they are the heights he can take you to before, inevitably because of

his character, just dropping you completely. A devastating snub, withering glance or acerbic rebuke that is lethal from over 100 yards. But that is the alter ego of Masson and today it is Masson the marvellous, magical and mercurial. No better midfield player in this division when he is in this mood. And we are all grateful since he knows as well as we do that he is performing on a different plane. He needs the likes of Brindley and Stubbs for a spot of protection and the oiks such as me, the Bolt and to a lesser extent Archie Mann to fetch and carry while he works his magic. And in the 4-3-3 formation, he struts around with those little legs to great effect in the capital. Every pass, a considered one, crafted and seldom wasted. "You love this ball, you must caress it as if you're fucking making love to it," Jimmy would urge in training and Masson carried out the instruction to the full. Orient, who beat us by a country mile at Meadow Lane last year, are still in with a squeak near the top of the league. Solid, promotion material with Barrie Fairbrother, Ricky Heppolette and Gerry Queen driving them on. But we are able to match them on the day and Masson - who else - scores the equaliser to make it 1-1. Back at the party, we are gathered to watch the game on the old black and white in the kitchen on Match of the Day. Masson has the starring role, me a small walk-on part. Blink and you missed it.

Monday, April 22

A win double tonight! Watched the reserves beat Halifax Town 6-0 at Meadow Lane. Dire, dreadful Halifax. Bring your boots and have a trial with Halifax.

They must have picked up the back four as hitchhikers on the way down. The North Midlands League can be a desperate affair at times. Take away Sunderland and Middlesbrough and precious little remains of appeal. Particularly a wet and windy Tuesday night earning a crust by turning out against Halifax Reserves at The Shay, that feared venue where Willie Carlin confirmed that his bite was as fierce as his bark. He played there for our Stiffs one night so the story goes and was taking dire abuse from one of the ten men and his dog who had bothered to check on the form of their local second XI in what passed for a main stand. Anyway, wee Willie, veteran of Leicester City and Derby County promotion campaigns, couldn't stand it any longer and jumped over the railings and responded in kind, face to face, with his biggest fan. Willie has gone to Cardiff City now but not before he had ensured another promotion with Notts and made an instant impression on me. He reduced me to tears one night against Scunthorpe ressies during early days at Meadow Lane, calling me everything from a pig to a dog and advising me to seek an alternative career, perhaps in the Inland Revenue. Not quite so eloquently but I know he meant well. Character building he called it. Character demolition more like and I still thought he was an evil, embittered old pro whose legs had gone and he envied my youth. But then Willie was entitled. I used to watch him, turning up like model pro on two counts, in that he was a fine example to us all and that he was attired like a dummy from John Collier's display window, early for the reserve games that were his lot in life now. All four

foot nothing of seething aggression on the pitch. He would get undressed and sit in front of the old electric fire in the corner of the home team dressing room. A sight to behold indeed was Willie, his shorts and shirt on but no socks, laying back and massaging his ankles in all the warmth that the two dark orange bars, working full out, could muster. Bandy legged, walking like a cripple across the cold linoleum, it was hard to imagine the fear and awe he could generate once this pint-sized Scouser was let loose on a football pitch. And the other part of the double? A result back at Gillott's Close. It wasn't pretty and she offered as much resistance as Halifax Reserves but there was no way I could score more than once.

Tuesday, April 23

My first chance to make the programme pen pictures and I have blown it. Dennis Marshall, the secretary, handed me a form the other week to fill in a few personal details. I didn't want it to be the Steak Diana Ross cliché - favourite food: Steak Diane; favourite singer: Diana Ross; favourite movie star: Paul Newman; favourite film: Butch Cassidy and the Sundance Kid. No I wanted to be different. So I put the Applejacks as favourite singers, Sugar Sugar as favourite record and The Magic Roundabout as favourite television programme. I thought it was clever; Dennis thought otherwise. "If you don't take the form seriously why should I bother to take the reply seriously," he said when I asked why my profile had not been in the programme. Silly old sod.

Thursday, April 25

Brindley is on the prowl for Cup final tickets. He offers well over the odds for mine, which I gladly accept. Says they are all going to his family and friends. Yes Billy. The fleet of cars depart for training this morning to Wilford Tip. There are various car schools ferrying players up there, Vint, Paul Dyer, known as Sammy, and the Bolt are all younger pros who take it in turn to drive the apprentices. Sammy, a stocky central midfield player, is full of honest endeavour and a fair amount of ability but he is not one of the gaffer's favourites. Ronnie would pick him in the first team in a shot, or so he tells him but Sammy is far from a jewel in Jimmy's crown. I didn't understand why, when we were called back for extra training in the afternoon, which usually meant laps around the track, Sammy would disappear shortly before the dreaded task began. "Nerves," the Bolt said. "Gone to the crapper."

He didn't suffer from them when driving to and from Meadow Lane although anyone travelling as a passenger with the Bolt was certain to suffer from lack of oxygen. The cigarette lighter and what was most likely the 20th fag of the day was lit up by the time he had got to the end of the Main Stand. It must have been his 20th because he walked into training always with a filter tip on the go. Walked, no more waddled like a penguin even though there was not an ounce of fat on him. His lungs must be terrible but he remains just about the fastest over 20 yards, barring Nixo perhaps, in the club.

Today Sammy is driving his Bedford van with the loose side door, a vehicle he uses to deliver groceries and eggs during a spot of afternoon moonlighting on his way home to Leicester. The trip to Wilford is always a sedate one but the return journey not quite so. It normally involves a mad dash, Dick Dastardly-style, back to Meadow Lane. The older pros tend not to lower themselves but the Bolt, in his Triumph 2000, and Sammy often race to see who is first back to base. On one occasion, Sammy 'winged' an old woman as she crossed the road but no charges were brought against him. It has not deterred him and today the two of them have set off along Wilford Lane at speed, cutting up traffic and nipping in and out of slower cars on the busy single lane road. Lights at the junction of Loughborough Road bring them level then it's off and over Trent Bridge and onto Arkwright Street before a dangerous chicane brings them onto London Road and the final lap right to the Cattle Market and Meadow Lane.

Following just behind, the two are neck and neck with the Bolt just edging it. At the bend of Arkwright Street, there is a petrol station that leads onto London Road. Sammy spots his chance and as a bewildered customer is filling up his tank on the forecourt, Sammy whizzes by in his light blue resprayed Bedford and nudges ahead in the race.

It is a daring move that wins the day but if Jimmy ever found out, Sammy's already dubious future career in football would be curtailed pretty swiftly.

Friday, April 26

Bought four copies of the Newark Advertiser. Photo flattering. Looked slim. Made some presentations at school in the afternoon. Brian McKinney, who was manager of my old South Nottingham Under-11s, asked me to do it and I was glad to help. It took me back to Milford Junior School, long summer evenings playing football on the school field and even longer winter nights playing Relivio or roaming the streets trying to smash street lamps or some such nonsense. A meal in the evening at the Black Boy for Lee Merrin, my best mate, who is emigrating to New Zealand next week. Collier has gone home for more lager and sex in Macclesfield. By one in the morning back at Gillott's Close, I am thoroughly depressed.

Monday, April 29

Bristol City beaten 2-1 on Saturday. The season is over now - finished 10th in the league although we had the chances to be up there. Luton, with 50 points, sneak second spot behind Middlesbrough. Worst of all, though, Forest are seventh, two points ahead. Enough mindless statistics.

Grandad is in hospital for an operation to remove cancer cells. The granite hands, honed from a lifetime's manual labour at Workington steelworks and on the Manchester docks, are trembling in the City Hospital. Grandma is also ill, frail and worried sick back home in Clifton. Life is a shambles, so bloody unjust. The rest doesn't matter.

Merrin has flown to New Zealand. Played Foxtrot by Genesis in tribute and shed tears all night long.

Tuesday, April 30

Training is awful but then we are preparing for the Nottinghamshire County Cup, an albatross that hangs around the necks of professional footballers when the real season is over. The Notts FA insists that part-timers like Arnold Town are not allowed to join in so that means Mansfield Town, Forest and ourselves must delay all hope of an early holiday. Forest are the holders so we are playing Mansfield, of the Fourth Division, tomorrow night. There is no conviction in preparation. Limbs are tired or tedious but for Stubbo and Co there is the post-training bacon sarnie at Jo's café, on the corner of Meadow Lane, to inspire them through another session. In my first pre-season as a pro last summer, there was always a pint of milk waiting after the morning session, a good healthy energy provider, then after the afternoon stint, the senior pros would dash off to dirty Jo's for a greasy bacon cob and several cups of equally foul and greasy tea. Purely habit and generations of County players, including Lawton, have been coming here over the decades. Forest, too, have Trent Bridge café with views over the Shire Hall and the river where the apprentices and senior pros religiously have their bacon butties or beans on toast. Still, if it detains someone, a Probey or Brindley perhaps, from pub duty, then it has served a useful purpose.

Wednesday, May 1

Mansfield are beaten 4-2 but it is no thanks to me. I played as I prepared, lazily. A loose pass let in Dick Edwards, the guitar-playing centre half who has aspirations in the world of showbusiness, and after leading comfortably by two goals, it was game on even if it was anything but as far as I was concerned.

Masson is on the case now. "Are you playing tonight, son?" I turn and offer a smile.

"I'll fucking make sure you never play for this club again son," he responds. Several minutes later, I am off for an early bath.

"Don't worry about it," The Claw and Braddy comfort me later over a pint. But I was upset, which was after all the intention of the remark.

Saturday, May 4

Both grandparents in hospital now. Grandma in the General but we can't tell grandad - yet. Please God, let them pull through. Liverpool beating Newcastle United in the FA Cup final occupies the brain and fills the mind with inanities. MacDonald doesn't get a kick which is great news for the quiet souls of football.

Monday, May 6

Selected in first team for the County Cup final at the City Ground tonight. Driving in from Bingham with a car park ticket at an away ground was really strange. It's usually

by coach and with my jacket hung up in the back, then showing my pass at the gate, there is an air of independence and importance which is undeserving of the occasion. Dangerous, seductive stuff this fame business, even at this parochial level. But I can handle it. Give me more and please, some glamorous women to go with it! It seems an age ago when I caught the bus back to Clifton after we were beaten by Forest on Boxing Day last year. The first Nottingham derby for 15 years and we lost to a dubious George Lyall penalty after Needham had tripped McKenzie just outside the area. Well it looked that way. 33,000 fans wedged into Meadow Lane, its wooden stands creaking at the weight. No chance of fiddling the gate receipts that day with the Spion Kop brimming to overflow with Forest fans. I was replacing the rock-like Stubbo (a few weeks before he'd copped for a six-studded challenge to the groin by Souness of Middlesbrough that was two days late and inflated his testicles to the size and colour of a crown green bowl) and didn't do too bad up against Neil Martin and McKenzie. Passengers on the purple South Notts 68 bus home didn't agree. "First thing he's stopped all afternoon," came a voice from the back of the queue when I stuck my hand out on Arkwright Street to catch the bus. Tired, bruised and aching from the intensity of the derby match, it was the last thing I needed, particularly as the caustic comment could well have been delivered by a Notts fan.

With trepidation I trudged upstairs clutching my black kit bag with 'Notts County' emblazoned in white across the front, sitting on the front seat among the smokers, hoping to disappear in the smog on the top deck during the half hour journey home to Clifton Estate. "We don't half miss Stubbsy," was the first comment that came into earshot from somewhere behind. "Beam me up Scotty," didn't work then and a slow, painful trip on a dark, chilly winter's night unfolded. It was the same number bus that had deposited me on London Road at 8.30pm five months earlier, reporting for my first day of work on the day school was out forever (apologies for blatant plagiarism Alice). Over an hour and a quarter early for training, I lingered two stops beyond the Meadow Lane bus stop and wandered lonely as a clown really, attempting to kill time by absorbing the fumes of rush hour traffic on London Road and taking in the sights of grown men fishing in the canal on a steaming hot July morning.

Now, almost a year on in the heat and twilight of a summer's evening, I was making a more assured grand entrance among the hoi polloi at Forest in my gleaming white Fiat. Well it seemed that way.

We lost 3-2 but it was a farcical game and John Robertson had a good word for me afterwards which cheered me up no end. "Keep dinking them in there, David, and you can make that left-sided midfield position your own." It was nice of Robbo to say so. Robbo, apart from Arthur Mann, the nicest Scotsman in the game. Like all his compatriots he has a weakness for a wee tipple or three but unlike most of them, he doesn't want to fight the world after two shandies. Robbo's inebriation is gentle and harmless and since his alter ego is Bryan Ferry, it can also be quite entertaining observing him deteriorate to his own renditions of Virginia Plain complete with all the

dress sense and mannerisms of the Roxy Music guru. Since he drinks at the city's first and trendiest wine bar, it is not an act that I catch frequently, preferring to slum it with the Camra anoraks and real ale buffs at the Newmarket Hotel across the other side of Hockley.

Thursday, May 9

Brown envelope day. £19.83 which is slightly different from the 76 quid you can draw with a couple of bonuses. Strapped for cash so borrowed £2 from the club's kitty. Mr Marshall will ensure it is paid back. The Player of the Year dance at the Sherwood Rooms, one of Nottingham's dance halls where the big bands have come and gone over the years. A captive audience for Amazing Grace and her associates; the mole, the wart or the one who looks like a bloke in drag. It's a dilemma to be sure for every red-blooded professional. Collier grabs two of the Golden Girls, who sell the golden goal tickets for the half time draw at the Lane. Their number comes up tonight.

Friday, May 10

Last day of training. Weigh in on the scales, a shade under 13 and a half stone. Not bad; not great. You are allowed a couple of pounds slack during the summer but anything over that and it is a fiver for every pound, a reasonable incentive to drink less and play more squash in the summer. Celebrate with a few pints at the Fairham Hotel, my old local at Clifton.

Eat your heart out Georgie Boy.
Miss World, or Miss Notts County? No contest.
Impressed, from left are: Randall and Hopkirk, alias Eric Probert
and David Needham; John Sims, Myself and Dave Smith - with
shirt collars awaiting clearance from Air Traffic Control.
Miss Notts County is being attended by Pedro Richards and a
bouquet of flowers.

Sunday, May 12

Reflection on a first season in professional football:
Bad Habits of professional footballers:
1) Urinating in the bath
2) Urinating over hair when washing it
3) Urinating over body when washing it
4) Dumping in bath when you are under water rinsing
hair, emerging to turd floating close to nostrils
5) Throwing hot tea over naked body
6) Pressing hot spoon against penis

Bad Habits of apprentices:
1) Stealing clothes which are returned within three months
2) Tying knots in clothing
3) Telling lies i.e. you are wanted on the phone when relaxing in bath
4) Many of the above

Tomorrow: managers and directors

Monday, May 13

Bad Habits of manager:
1) Extracting urine as in: How does it feel to be a star, eh, David after I received good press for performance at Roker Park on New Year's Day
2) Swearing and cussing at everyone except the little man, the jewel, eh
3) Blaming me for death of Churchill, etc
Bad Habits of directors
1) Picking noses and acting superior
2) Extracting further urine regarding my a) sandals b) ties, lack of them mostly c) trousers d) shirts e) jackets f) hair etc

Friday, May 17

Finished Puckoon this morning, in fits of laughter by the end. Something of a contrast to the afternoon spent at the ABC cinema, queueing up in bright sunshine to see The Exorcist. People distributing leaflets and emergency

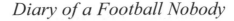

phone lines in case of distress. It is only a film, for goodness sake.

Sunday, May 19

Played cricket for Stapleford with some of my old schoolteachers. Great excuse for an afternoon in the sun and a session in The Feathers pub at night. Drove home after eight pints of Home Ales to Bingham and caught M.A.S.H. Awake at 3.25am on the settee. Collier has returned home for the summer and I crawl up to my bedroom which has a pane of glass above the door through which you can see the entrance to the roof loft. Is there scratching up above?

Friday, May 24

I have tried every remedy known to man to induce a good night's sleep, including sampling several pints of Stella Artois, 28p a pint, in the Beehive pub at Maplebeck with Paul, my brother who drinks for the world XI. It is all to no avail because every time I get up into that bedroom, the street lamp shines directly onto that pane of glass, illuminating the loft trapdoor. Occasionally a freight train passes by on the nearby railway line to cheer me up but in general, I have been bloody terrified this last week, recalling The Exorcist and its chilling plot which was told so mundanely. No creaking doors in Cornish taverns or Christopher Lee talking through fanged teeth. It was the feasibility of it all that has remained to haunt me, literally, this week. Waking every half hour to see that loft and

listen intently for rodents or otherwise scrambling about up there. And my only friend in the world being my old transistor, brought with me from Clifton but which can still pick up Radio Luxembourg or any station that broadcasts in English beyond the witching hour. That and the sheets that make me invisible to demons on the prowl. Oh for Christ's sake. I analyse myself and the situation in the light of day. The whole thing is preposterous, I know but come the dark . . .

Monday, May 27

"So what did you do during the close season, son?" I can imagine Jack or Jimmy asking in July. Well there I was on this camping trip to the Lake District over bank holiday weekend with my brother. We'd downed a few the night before in the Swan at Buttermere and then set off at the foot of Ennerdale for a full day's hike. Decked out in Spanish fell boots, Notts County training top and sunglasses I make it to the top of one of the hills when the mist and fog descend. We nudge precariously along a ridge, visibility is just a few feet and we are fearful that our supplies of cheese and pickle cobs and bar of chocolate might not be sufficient. Suddenly there is the sound of a man running, and at a good clip; we are passed by a fell runner, in shorts and vest, speeding by our stumbling frames and into the distance to what appears a sheer drop of several hundred feet. Perhaps alerting mountain rescue teams is a touch dramatic after all.

In our contracts, we are forbidden to ride motorcycles or mopeds but it doesn't say anything about being

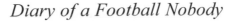

prohibited from risking life and limb at the summit of a rocky crag with Cumberland fell runners in close attendance. Does it, boss?

Thursday, June 13

In winter or in summer, the girls and boys of Greenholme School can be an insufferable lot but today, a spot of cricket and netball practice has kept them occupied. Nixo is back in charge. Quite rightly too, since he is a former teacher, one of those who did his teacher training and kept playing the professional game. A superb athlete, tremendous acceleration and spring that takes him beyond players at ease. Considered a bit too bright for his own good sometimes in that he can be obdurate, deliberately so, when Jimmy wants more of him. Ultimately, there will be only one winner but Nixo seems oblivious to that. In conversations with him, it doesn't bother him. He wants two or three more moves before his career ends, picking up a few grand in signing-on fees for each one and a bit of cash-in-hand when leaving. He has it all planned out.

Eric Mac will be earning a more lucrative crust with a summer job like Arthur Mann. Archie, the battery boy who runs all day and night. The most likeable Scotsman you will ever meet and a devoted family man. Even so, for the sake of team spirit, he always makes it to a night club after an away game for a few drinks. "You bloody man, Brindley," he will say having been persuaded to head for Babel or the 99 after

Steak...Diana Ross

the obligatory five pints of lager at the TBI. He is mimicking Jack, of course, but, as in most things in Arthur's life, without a trace of malice.

How on earth some of the other married men get away with it so regularly is astonishing. Either the players' wives failed miserably at geography in school or their perception of time is not what it should be. Or more likely they turn a blind eye to the schoolboy shenanigans. We are usually back in Nottingham sitting in the TBI with a nearly empty glass of lager by 8.30pm after a game in London, not 10.30pm as some tell their better halves. Night games are different, normally a dash from the car park up town to catch the last dregs, of beer and women, before the 2pm shut-down.

Arthur is usually long gone before then, often with Masson. The odd couple? Maybe. The two are the best of friends and the best of enemies. Like chalk and cheese in characters but then opposites do attract even if on the pitch Arthur, normally mild mannered Archie, is driven to the point of taking a swing at the wee man who sits sedately in the middle of the park chastising the pit ponies, Arthur and me, for not chasing one of his more errant passes with sufficient enthusiasm.

Worse still, he can turn the crowd against us, a look to the heavens and then back at Arthur. "They are not even fit to chase decent passes," the posture is telling his woes to the terraces.

But Arthur can put his medals on the table. A League Cup one with Manchester City, playing then as a left back or sweeper, calm and calculated at the back and his best position, unlike the more frenetic demands of midfield where Arthur's pace and stamina makes him indispensable to the Sirrel strategy and if Masson did but know it, his too.

We have all heard the story of Arthur's fear of flying and how the plane he was on with Manchester City had to turn around and drop him off at Manchester airport, so ill was he by a combination of pills, alcohol and the sheer terror of being 20,000 feet above the ground. And now in summer, he will partner Eric Mac on a building site, digging trenches and shifting muck and mud for £25 a week, cash in hand, to supplement his £40 a week basic with Notts and make up for the absence of a win bonus for two months. It will help the McManus and Mann households. And here I am trying to relay the technique of batting to some of the most privileged children in Nottingham.

Friday, June 14

The summer diet that began a fortnight ago has not being going to plan. The crisps and chocolate biscuits have disappeared but the pints of beer have not. Worth a drink tonight, though, because Denis Law played in his first, and probably last, game in the World Cup finals. Scotland beat Zaire 2-0. The Claw nowhere to be seen in autograph hunt.

Saturday, June 22

A cause to celebrate for communists everywhere. East Germany 1 West Germany 0. Yippee. Trying to get to grips with cutting the lawn but domestic duties are not my calling this summer. Scotland out of World Cup even though they drew 1-1.

Saturday, July 6

Have just completed an assault course camping in Portmadoc, Wales. Six days of rain, rain, and more rain despite it being in a dry county on the Sunday we arrived. Thereafter a liquid diet every day. As penance, finally mowed the lawn today then watched Jimmy Connors demolish Ken Rosewall in the men's singles final at Wimbledon. Brash uncouth youth against the old order, a triumph of power and metal against the guile and the wooden racket. The end of an era. Janet Haynes brings sunshine and a Horse With No Name by America. The start of a new era? Forget it McVay.

Sunday, July 7

The Krauts beat Holland 2-1 in the World Cup final. Best team lost. Cruyff brilliant. Jack Taylor, the referee, wasn't bad either.

Monday, July 8

Collier returned to Bingham today. Two days to go before pre-season training begins. Tonight I meet a few mates in town and drink five slimline tonic waters. After two months of abusing the body with alcohol, fish and chips from the local chippie and several curries, this radical new regime will work wonders in just under 48 hours. Sucking the lemon assuages the feeling of hunger.

Wednesday, July 10

The great weigh-in for the great white whale. But all is well. No blubber, just under 13 and a half stone. Mind you Jack would have doctored the scales for me if he thought I was struggling. Ian Scanlon, Scotland's answer to Walter Mitty, has a huge chain and cross hanging around his neck, which mostly deters the women he has been known to meet in dark corners of even darker nightclubs. "Don't go on the scales wearing that, Scanny, it must weigh a ton," Bradd remarks, licking his lips in mock fashion because there is no danger of Scanny having put an ounce of weight on during the summer. Even so, Scanny obeys - and holds the chain in his hand as he mounts the scales and can't understand the laughter that ensues.

A fleet of cars takes us up through Sneinton, beyond Green's Windmill and the narrow streets of Sneinton Dale and its terraced housing, arriving at Colwick Woods, overlooking the racecourse and railway lines. A photo call for the Nottingham Evening Post and we are off into the bowels of the woods, up hills, down dales, doggies, piggy back races and all manner of exercise in the blazing sun. Ronnie is at the head of affairs with Jimmy. It is a gruelling session that always ends with a run up Pork Chop Hill, a deceiving slope of around half a mile that is the light at the end of the tunnel. It peaks, with lungs bursting and oxygen in short supply, into a tree-lined

opening that is virtually a sheer face and after that you collapse at the top, taking in air and gradually focusing on the cars on the road where you first arrived a good two hours earlier.

Then it is back to Wilford Tip, two pints of cold milk or cordial and we are re-acquainted with our old friend the football. Unusual to see one so early in pre-season but it is Jimmy's philosophy.

He stands Roy Brown and Eric Mac in the centre of a circle, the goalkeepers alternating as target practice in the middle. But first you have to drive a pass across the circle, straight to the feet of another player who controls it in one and whacks the bloody ball as hard as his aching and tired limbs will allow into Roy's midriff. There are two circles, one for the apprentices and others out of favour and one of the first team pool. It is only a matter of time before one of the passes goes astray in our company. The unfortunate miscreant is the Bolt. Jimmy pounces with a peep of the whistle, eyes bulging, chops expanding and saliva oozing from his mouth on this blistering afternoon. Small wonder he has been christened the Elephant Man by some of the senior ranks.

"Jesus fucking Christ, Ian. Give me that fucking ball, son," he is standing next to the Bolt. It was either him, me or Vint Jimmy was waiting for to make our mistake. He leaves the older pros to their own devices no matter. The gaffer is now prancing about the ball, tiptoeing around it in a manner that mocks the Bolt's attempts to hit a pass. In fact, when he connects, he has one of the hardest shots in the club.

"You love this fucking ball. Aye, you should caress the bloody thing," Jimmy is falling in love with the leather orb all over again. "Steady on boss," Bradd pipes up. "Jesus Christ Wesley, you could be making love to it. But no back scuttling, eh, eh, eh, eh." Jimmy has dissolved into laughter at his own humour, the large protruding tooth dominating his infectious laugh. He turns to the Bolt and strokes his hair. He's had his moment. Seconds later, the ball is rolled out to the Bolt again. He hits another reasonable pass, similar to the previous one that incurred Jimmy's rage. "That's fucking better son. Now come on Billy, breen one in." Jimmy is fully animated on the fringes of the circle as Brindley controls the pass instantly and closes in to smash a shot up and over Eric Mac that is well on the way to the River Trent. Jimmy turns away and mutters to himself "Billy, tut, tut, Billy. Eh. That will never do." But it is not even a rebuke. He knows that Billy has run through brick walls for him. He knows the men from the boys.

Thursday, July 11

The sight of me and Collier hobbling, the strains and stiffness being a direct result of yesterday's exercise shock to the system, to my car in the morning must have amused the residents of Gillotts Close, a small cul-de-sac comprised of Wimpey homes built in the mid-1960s located just on the fringes of Bingham. It was once a small village about eight miles east of Nottingham which is rapidly expanding to accommodate those with loftier ideals in life. They are a decent bunch; our neighbour even lent us his petrol-driven lawnmower when he saw me struggling valiantly against the jungle in our front garden armed only with a manual mower and not a lot of man at that. Even so, I bet they will be glad when we are gone simply because of the parties and comings and goings in the dead of night that have occurred in the short time since we moved in. All married with children, they seem an ancient lot with their lives all mapped out.

They will probably have their wish soon. It is not working out between Collier and me even after he had been back home all summer, there is an air in the house. He will probably go back into digs and do his shagging away from home and I will return to Clifton where my grandparents are both struggling with their health. Pat, my mum, and Peggy, my aunt, are trying their best but there are problems at home. I might be best being there at the moment.

Training was bloody hard today. Sweat rash around the groin didn't help. The afternoon session was pure hell, endless laps and relays around the cricket pitch. They are meat and drink to the likes of Benjy, Tristan Benjamin, the young West Indian apprentice and a fine athlete. He runs gracefully, effortlessly for most of the day, hardly seeming to draw breath. In the dressing room he is as quiet as a church mouse. The senior pros try to draw him out of his shell with some suitably witty remarks but Benjy goes a little deeper than most one suspects.

Friday, July 12

Stiff as a board today. Our first practice match and I am playing centre half in the reserves. Clearly not in first team

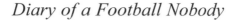

plans this year. But at least enjoyed being back in the centre of defence even if trying to win a header off big Braddy is nigh on impossible. He jumps broad and hangs in the air brilliantly so when Eric Mac is kicking the ball long from his hands, he wins just about every flick-on. It makes me realise what you have to compete against if you are going to succeed, even at Second Division level, week in, week out. "That's the key, David, consistency," Jack is telling me in the treatment room after the game, trying to sort out my bloody irritating rash. On the two tables in the tiny room just off the dressing room, little Smithy is reclining on his back in the nude with only a towel to cover up his private parts. It is a penis to which his right arm has become fondly attached, a relationship he willingly demonstrates in the smaller bath in the away team dressing room. In Jack's little room, though, Jack's rules apply and much as Smithy would love to show off his ability to flick his penis swiftly into the erect position, both his right and left hands remain idle at the side of the bed.

He took a knock in the practice match on his ankle and a sun lamp that appears to have been a prop in one of those old Flash Gordon movies is transmitting heat into the swollen area around the ankle bone.

Jimmy has left the ground early today, most probably hiking it up to Scotland in his Austin 40, an eight hour drive to some god-forsaken outback to spy on a Scottish junior player who will be the next Denis Law or Billy Bremner.

It is a precarious trip for him and other road-users; he is far from the best driver even though he was, according

to himself, one of the best outside rights to emerge from north of the border when he moved from Celtic to Aldershot.

"You cannee fucking take the ball away from me big fellow," he once gibed towards Stubbo on a rain-sodden surface at Chilwell Army Depot, goading him to make a tackle. Of course, Stubbo could well have sent him over the barracks if he had connected but conditions and commitment were not in Stubbo's favour and his sliding tackle missed by a mile, leaving the gaffer to bob and weave his way merrily down the right wing, duping imaginary defenders along the way. And then just as quickly as he entered fantasy island, he would depart.

"Aye, this fancy dan stuff, jigging and jagging, it's no fucking good at all unless you can breen that ball in at the end, eh," and he was making a point with his hand on hip and walking back towards the touchline. 'Breen it in' being akin to 'breech it in' and 'scud the fucking thing in' in Sirrel-speak which all amounted to delivering a decent final ball. And he hoped it would sink in, to Carter, Scanlon, me and anyone else who found a precious yard of space down the touchline or near the byline.

"Now let's play, eh. Blow that fucking whistle Jackson," and with that Jack would re-start the practice match, normal service was resumed and Jimmy wandered off to the touchline confident of making a good point and that his reputation as one of Scotland's finest was unimpaired. Except that Brindley had found a cutting in an old newspaper, sent to him by a mate, which read that, in one game while playing for Celtic, Sirrel had been a 'liability on the wing'.

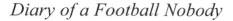

"A liability, it's there in black and white," Brindley beamed although he stopped short of pinning the clipping up on the notice board.

There is a score to settle for Brindley, here. "But boss, it wasn't me, it was Stubbo," he had told Jimmy after Notts had lost a vital promotion game against Aston Villa a couple of seasons ago. I remember it on Match of the Day at the time, County hit the bar, the post and missed a penalty and should have won easily in front of a packed Villa Park. Instead Villa won 1-0 and went onto promotion from the Third Division when Ray Graydon, probably the smallest bloke on the pitch, crept in at the far post to head the winner. Jimmy was convinced it was Billy's fault and had him defending long crosses at the far post for the rest of the week. "I told him to look at the action replay. It was bloody Stubbs. Couldn't get a fag paper between him and the ground." And Stubbo still laughs about his escape but Brindley's fate is the same as Doc Daneeka in Catch-22. He is the dead man at the far post even though all the evidence, i.e. that he is alive and kicking in at the near post, suggests otherwise.

But today Jimmy is away and for a little while Jack can play - nervously. Even with the gaffer approaching Hadrian's Wall, Jack speaks in hushed tones and raised eyebrows and furtive glances to the door of the treatment room, expecting Jimmy to loom large at the entrance. One of the old school who played in goal either side of the war for Birmingham City and then in an Huddersfield team that set a record of having the back three as ever-presents in a promotion season in the 1950s, he knows his place in modern football. Jack is up there with Andy Beattie, one

of the nicest blokes in the game who has been with Notts since Tommy Lawton brought him as coach in 1957.

He talks of his time as caretaker manager when the side were unbeaten in countless games; Smithy eggs him on to stories closer to the bone, trying to draw a hint of disaffection from him, but Jack has none of it, even in this very private audience. "Trust nobody in this game, David." It is Jack's motto and he is, as always, right.

Eventually, after several requests, he finally gets out his ukulele, hidden in a secret place somewhere down the corridor. "When I'm leaning on the lamppost on the corner of the street . . ." There is only me and the apprentices, leaning on their mops, to appreciate a rather twitchy George Formby impersonation at Meadow Lane.

Friday, July 19

We have probably seen the last of Colwick Woods for another year after a grueller of a morning up there yesterday. The legs are less heavy now but how Jack keeps going round in the heatwave is remarkable. There was a full scale practice match today. I played in the first team but only because Stubbo was injured. Enjoyable, though, and words of praise from Masson. He's been different again this week and he has invited me back to his house and tennis club at Burton Joyce for a game of tennis this afternoon. Masson the Merciless has gone for now; long live Masson the Marvellous even if Braddy tells the story that when he was beating him at tennis, Masson walked off in a huff and took the balls with him.

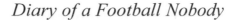

"They're mine and I'm going home," Braddy told it mockingly. But what a house Masson has at Burton Joyce, one of the more fashionable Nottingham suburbs. Seems huge and rambling. Arthur Mann and the Claw come for a game of doubles later. Great afternoon. Should I join the club? Now there's a thought. Does the four bedroomed' mansion come with membership?

Memo diary: My love life is crap. Two girlfriends have both ditched me simultaneously.

Tuesday, July 23

Stubbo still injured so got the nod for our first friendly of the season, away to Birmingham City at their training ground. Very hot, but very good 2-1 win despite Kenny Burns, their centre forward, being tipped as a Scottish striker for the future.

Needham had him in his pocket from start to finish. For a First Division side they didn't shape too well but then pre-season friendlies are not a good form guide for the real thing.

Packed up and left Bingham at the weekend, returned to Clifton and Collier to digs. It is much better now for the pair of us except I am back in a rut at home. And the mickey taking in the dressing room is rife. "Lover's tiff is it then," Vint has his say before everyone else chimes in. "You'll have to kiss and make up eventually. It takes time. These things do." Bastards.

Steak...Diana Ross
Saturday, July 27

Peterborough United away at London Road. Lost 2-1 but played well. Centre half to start with then midfield in the second half. Played Nixo in for our goal: "Just keep doing that, Davie boy, and you'll be fine.' Archie is encouraging. Masson, who I beat at tennis the previous day, is also in fine form. I am at one with the world. If only I could crack the code and the meaning of life with the opposite sex.

Tuesday, July 30

Beat Lincoln City at Sincil Bank behind closed doors. An easy win and switched once again to midfield in the second half. Does this bode well for the start of the season? In the afternoon I picked little Smithy up to have a walk about town with the apprentices. He lives with his mum and dad and sister in the old part of The Meadows that has not, as yet, been demolished. Shades of Coronation Street only more cramped, and they still share an outside loo in the yard with three other neighbours. Makes Clifton Estate positively regal in comparison. He's waiting upstairs, getting ready to 'chike' - that is wandering around town ogling after women twice his age hoping for a dalliance or more. We are standing in the kitchen. "Can't go yet, there's a woman coming around to collect some eggs me mam left her." He explains who the woman is, a prostitute who he claims to have taken from the rear in hugely entertaining circumstances. The 'back scuttling' method to which the gaffer referred, doubtless.

"I got her to put some chips in the oven and warmed up the two front rings of the hob, to keep her tits warm. Yer loved it m'duck didn't you." He is re-living the alleged encounter with the lady now for she has now come to collect her eggs. "Gerroff you dirty little bleeder," she responds. She is laughing and revealing tobacco stains in between her teeth. The hair is bleached blonde. She must be 50 at least. Even from behind it could not have been an attractive proposition.

Later that night Smithy is trying it on again, with Pat, a woman of similar age who is the landlady of the Railway Hotel. She and her husband John run the Centenary Bar at Meadow Lane and they often throw a dance and invite the players along to support the cause and meet the regulars in Netherfield. A smashing couple whose interior is adorned with wall-to-wall pictures of Notts County for the past 20-odd years or more. Smithy is chatting up Pat; I'm throwing up in the toilets and everyone ends up pretty pissed. I end up where I started, taking Smithy home. A pip goodnight and 50 yards down the road, two uniformed policeman shine a light to slow me down on the cobbled street. The sergeant leans in through the window. After my Railway Hotel vomit, I have sobered up considerably but the car reeks of beer.

"No need to make that sort of noise at this time of night, is there young man," Dixon of Dock Green says. "Do you live around here?" "No, I'm heading back to Clifton. Just dropped off Dave Smith, an apprentice at Notts County." "I see. We're just looking for someone in this area. Drive on home and mind how you go." Who says our policemen aren't wonderful?

Wednesday, July 31

Out with a couple of old schoolfriends in the King John in town when in walked Probey, all alone in his trusty white suit, a striking resemblance to one half of Randall and Hopkirk deceased. He just came out on his own to have a few drinks so I tagged along. There is a gloomier side to Probey and he is hard to fathom but I'm glad I kept him company before dropping him off at the bus station. He refused a lift home. It made me feel important, listening to the troubles of an older pro, but the following day it is all forgotten and he is part of the senior first team pack once again. That is the code of dressing room.

ERIC PROBERT:

If his career path had led him to tread the thespian boards, Theakston's Old Peculiar would have been Probey's stage name. A powerhouse midfield player and power drinker - and a talented footballer into the bargain.

Friday, August 2

Tour of West Country commences. Three matches in a week based at Exeter University. Trouble at mill to start with because there are no card tables on the coach. Bradd, Stubbs and Brindley are not happy. Read The Bedsitting Room by Milligan on the way down, chuckling out loud. Arrived 4.20pm after six hours on the road and a stop at Bristol. Masson has organised a tennis tournament, playing doubles until late into the night. We are staying in the student dormitories on campus, communal kitchen and all. Great sporting facilities but even in the holidays, there are hordes of French graduates and American law students staying there.

Saturday, August 3

Drew 1-1 with Torquay United. Not in the team.

Monday, August 5

Jack has a quiet word with me. The gaffer wants me to go on a diet again. Bollocks. The fat lad is back. Training was long and tiresome, a lot of tactics with those out of favour providing fake defenders or just loitering without intent while the first team practise set-pieces and attacking corners. Coach into Exeter at night but we are thwarted in trying to see The Three Musketeers at the cinema. On a wet and drizzly Monday night, there are 'house full' notices outside. They are easily pleased in Exeter, obviously.

Tuesday, August 6

Beat Exeter City 2-0. They were all kick and rush, which you might expect from a Fourth Division team. Their clumsy offside trap, a cavalry charge to the halfway line, was the most sophisticated tactic. Played the entire second half and should have scored when Vint's pass beat the trap. Raced on with only the goalkeeper left but screwed final shot wide. "You used to be a big, strong lad when you first came into the team," Mick, one of the office lads at Meadow Lane, told me later. "Now, well, you are just big." Thanks Mick. Spending your holiday down here following County says a lot about you, pal. He wasn't being malicious. Even so, I feel overweight tonight back on campus. One drink in the bar and back to the dorm. Knackered. Sleep.

Wednesday, August 7

In his capacity as a former PE teacher, Nixo is determined to teach me how to dive into the swimming pool properly. "It could come in handy in the penalty area in the unlikely event of you getting in there David." He had a way with words, did Nixo. So we spent an hour freezing our nuts off at the side of the outdoor pool, rain pelting down with an attractive swimming instructor for company. When she arrived, Nixo rather lost heart in the job in hand. Result: Banged head on the side of the pool underwater before desperately pushing away thinking it was the bottom. Nixo doubled up but unconcerned that I was close to

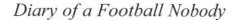

drawing my last breath. We were both in at the deep end but with different objectives. Pity she wasn't wearing a gas mask, Nixo.

Thursday, August 8

Tipping it down during training. Jimmy does not relent in his bollocking of me all morning. "That's just fucking awful, eh David," echoes around the campus playing fields like a flawed record that has got stuck on the needle. Perhaps if I could play it backwards like the White Album or Sergeant Pepper's it would tell me something meaningful. "Turn me on dead man" or "That's fucking brilliant, eh David." Trouble is, it can have a negative effect. I have got to the point that the ball is not my friend, I don't want to see it or receive it for fear of another rollicking. There are hiding places, in the hole or channel cunningly lurking between a marker and your own man. You can spend a quiet half hour failing to show for a colleague if you know what you are doing. It even happens on match days, not for so long but there have been occasions when even one or two of the senior pros are taking too much stick from the crowd and grab the invisible cloak for some respite. It is not spotted by the average fan but for the reserve lads sitting in the stands, it is noticed and pointed out gleefully among the throng. For Masson this morning, the message is straightforward. "Oh, good thinking little fellow," or "Bad luck little fellow." Even the 'little fellow' is finding it tiresome. He has that sheepish grin and laugh about him that can endear him to the rest of us. Teacher's pet without needing to take an apple because he passes the hardest of tests blindfolded. No revising, just sheer instinct and ability. And in his own way, when he deliberately fucks up and gets another "Not to worry little fellow" from Jimmy, he turns around to us all with a mocking face as if to say he can't lose.

An evening of television in the main lounge, The Goodies and Top of the Pops providing the contrast to the news bulletins about Richard Nixon at night. Shades of the East Midlands airport departure lounge with bodies everywhere, mostly the American students, awaiting news of Nixon's departure because of the Watergate scandal. Jimmy walks in and sees Brindley and Bradd at the bar with a glass of Coke each. "Good boys," he says, patting them on the head. He can't smell the rum on their breath. Then he can't find a seat and ends up kicking a massive 7ft Yankee in the thigh. "Hey George, move," he yells diplomatically. It becomes even more surreal as we are engaged in conversation about the political state of the American nation. Step forward Raymond O'Brien, Irish sage, who calls it the Watercloset scandal and puts an end to all debate.

There are queues outside Ian Scanlon's room in the dorm later. A young student couple going hell for leather on the bed in their room diagonally opposite but lower down. Voyeurism rules. We all agree: nine out of ten for star quality and presentation.

Friday, August 9

Nixon resigns. A 1-1 draw away with Swindon Town on our way home concludes the tour of the West Country.

Monday, August 12

Training then an afternoon of tennis in West Bridgford with a former Cambridge Blue at the sport was perhaps not the best way to prepare for the friendly at Sutton Town tonight. It is only a reserve XI against a bunch of part-timers from north of the county. This will be a doddle. It is, 5-2 but I have a touch of cramp and need treatment on the sidelines and finish with socks rolled down and hair, far too long, all over the place. Jimmy is not amused.

Tuesday, August 13

There is retribution for last night. Extra laps after training supervised by Ronnie. At least he takes pity on me as I struggle badly on the last of six timed runs. Jimmy tells me I am a disgrace, showing the paying public at Sutton that a professional footballer is not fit for a pre-season friendly. Brindley bucks me up with some advice. Advice, mainly good, everywhere seems to be falling on deaf ears.

Wednesday, August 14

Another reserve outing, at Burton Albion. No tennis in the afternoon this time and no cramp. Won 4-3, wee Willie Carlin was at the game. Found out that Steve Buckley, who I played with at Ilkeston Town in the

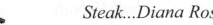

Southern League, had signed for Luton Town. He didn't stop long at the Manor Ground but then with his left foot, a blunderbuss of a weapon, he was always likely to have a chance at a higher level.

Thursday, August 15

The team sheet goes up for the first game of the season, at Bristol Rovers on Saturday. Not included, not even as the travelling reserve. Flash is named as substitute. Pissed off with the gaffer but then he has plenty of reasons to reciprocate the feeling.

Monday, August 19

A weekend of Nights in White Satin, ELO and Lindisfarne and a spot of Yes to ease the contemplation and find the meaning of life. It was not discovered down the Clifton Bridge Inn on Sunday lunchtime. Five pints of Home Ales helped with the search later, though, and a sighting of Pam Reynolds. Gaffer names the same team to play Fulham at Meadow Lane tomorrow night.

Time for gym work after training, a few stomachs and weights in Meadow Lane's brand new gymnasium which doubles for Peter Thompson's, the groundsman, tool shed. A hop and skip over the ride-on tractor, avoiding the trailer rakes and ploughs and the cans of petrol and weed killer, we can just about make it to the multi-gym that has been set up in the corner of the rotting old room at the far end of the Main Stand. When Jolly Jack Dunnett finally decides to torch the ground and claim on the insurance we all reckon the fire will, mysteriously, start here. Then watch that wooden stand go up along with JD's claim.

The out-of-favour crowd, the misfits, 'Sammy' Dyer, the Bolt, Vinter, little Smithy, Pedro and myself try to complete a circuit without interruption. It is not easy particularly with Smithy poking his finger, fresh from a journey deep into his bowels, boldly going where no fingers have gone before nor would want to, into your nostrils as you are coming up to do some sit-ups or trying to lift one of the ancient weights on the bar. Sometimes Jack will supervise, showing his dexterity at step-ups on the bench or how he still manages 40 sit-ups at nearly 60 years of age! He puts us all to shame.

Today, though, it is a volunteer crew. Smithy should know his way about the place at any rate. He claims to take his young admirers back under here after first team matches, having swept up in the dressing rooms and cleaned the baths, he reckons he meets them in the Centenary Bar before slipping out for some alternative push-ups and finger stretching routines.

If it is not Smithy "eyebrow raising exercises now lads, give me 50 double quick" stopping the show, then it is the unremitting dankness and coldness that brings the session to a premature halt. Either that or Peter, Concorde nose, swooping down and ranting and raving at the latest chore he has been asked to perform on the pitch by Jimmy.

"Too bloody long, what does he know about?" the groundsman storms in, oblivious to players at work in his domain. Peter maintains he keeps a pristine playing surface. There are no humps or hollows and certainly no bad bobbles. "It's your own fault if you can't control the

ball," he states with the air of a man who knows his argument will not be challenged.

Having sowed and reaped and cut his pitch into such good condition, why should clumsy idiots with studs on go and ruin it all. He really would prefer to watch the grass grow at Meadow Lane in preference to us play there.

Wednesday, August 21

My leg is five inches wider tonight after an old embittered bastard from Hull City reserves tried to break it. "Think what might have happened Macca if you hadn't been wearing pads," Brindley espouses as I receive treatment in Jack's room after the game. "He meant to break it all right, you mark my words son." It happened 20 minutes in and I should have seen it coming but the naivety of pursuing a lost cause in the penalty area rendered me blind to this nasty little shit who dived in below radar level and buried six studs in the shin bone. We won 1-0 and I played until the end and it didn't prevent me joining the rest of the team for the Wednesday evening thrash.

Tonight it ends, well nearly, at the Palais de Danse, scene of the revolving dance floor and revolving women, mostly married and in their forties and fifties. Grab-a-granny night and Smithy and Collier are in their element. There are others among us, playing away from home but on familiar ground in the Bali Hai; Vint and the Bolt, who have married young and have children and not yet 20 years old. There is the chance of a fleeting flirt; a quick grope behind the palm trees or better still a knee trembler beneath Trent Bridge (it is a popular retreat for the married lads, in walking distance from the 99 Club and anonymity is guaranteed for both parties. A bit of nookie in the night, al fresco. "Come up and see my etchings," Probey might say without fear of contradiction. For while she who can eat carrots through a tennis racket with her protruding teeth is thinking of England laid back against the granite stone of Trent Bridge arches, she can peruse the wit and wisdom and artistic quality of Kilroy who has passed this way many times before and recorded his passage in the most unusual corners and crannies up above).

Tonight from the Palais there are no such salubrious shagging quarters available. The rings will remain on their rightful place and the finger-wagging and recriminations of perfumed shirts or the tell-tale grazes on the knee from granite stone will be spared.

In Mansfield, it is unlikely to be so. The divorce rate among the married players there is probably the highest in the country, according to Colin Foster, their centre half. Of course, it is not the players' faults. You don't argue with a miner's wife when she is feeling randy, the old man is working his night shift down the pit and the collier's good lady is on the rampage in the plethora of pubs around Mansfield market place. "Life's too short to say no, yoerth," Fozzie insists, daring to mimic the distinctive drawl of the north Notts minefields that if attempted in the Squinting Cat pub on a collier's night out would mean a steady diet of liquidised hospital food for several weeks at the Mansfield Infirmary.

Still, they will be shagging tonight in the streets of Mansfield.

Tuesday, August 27

Denis Law retired today. Memo: must take down the posters in my bedroom. Another day, another practice match up Wilford Tip. There must be method to Jimmy's madness of training. Always a little 'chuke up' around the pitch with Ronnie before we launch into a full scale practice game. The older pros, Needham, Brindley, Bradd and Stubbs, the core of the side, moan constantly, complaining it is wearing them down, that fatigue is setting in and that we play five times more games than any other side in the Second Division - or the league for that matter.

Even when the reserves are absent, the gaffer arranges for the bibs to offer resistance to his irresistible tactics in an eleven-a-side contest. Last season, he had Jack laying out the yellow bibs at Wilford during February on the eve of a game away to Luton Town, trying to end a losing run of four games on the bounce. "Losing, it's like winning David, it becomes a habit son," Jimmy informed us on the Monday morning team talk. Then Jack took the bibs and set them down in a 4-4-2 formation, placing a brick or stone on top to stop them flying off in the gusting winds that seem to perpetually blow up what has been nicknamed 'the Hill' for no apparent reason.

"Jackson, Jackson! Put the fucking left back wider, aye that's it Jackson. Jesus Christ, let's have it right, eh," he mutters the last part under his breath. Right? Notts County's finest XI against a team of nylon yellow bibs. Right or normal isn't part of the equation, surely.

A surreal battle of wits begins with Bradd kicking off to Randall who then sprays his trademark driven pass out to the right wing for Nixo, who is in full flight from the kick-off whistle, to gather in his stride. For once, the Claw's passing is wayward. "Peep, peep," Jimmy can't get the whistle to his mouth quick enough as the pass limps over one of the bibs, slowing down Nixo in his run, who has to turn to retrieve the ball. "Jesus Christ, Kevin, that's no good at all, son." "But it's only a bib, boss," Nixo, standing with the ball at his feet now, remarks with that impish glint in his eye.

"Not a bit of it, Jon. That's Futcher or Aston, eh." (reference to Luton Town's finest).

So we start again. This time, the Claw gets it right, Nixo eases past the full back who is standing far too wide and is left for dead by his turn of pace. A low cross from the touchline and there is Braddy, skipping in between two static defenders to pounce with Jack standing in goal, the only opponent demonstrating visible signs of human life. "You bloody man, Bomber," Jack laughs, as Braddy dummies to blast one straight at him. Jack never flinches and Braddy taps home. During this unequal contest, the midfield are in support and the back four has pushed up to the halfway line in time-honoured fashion, urged on by Brindley's prompting across the line. "Come on back four, push up in unison now," he cajoles in a pompous accent, mocking the absurdity of the exercise. "Pick up that bib, McVay, and watch him in the air. Barry Butlin can still use his head a bit, son." There is laughter in the defensive ranks while up front Bradd, the Claw and Nixo are hugging one another after that clinical finish.

"Aye that's better, much better, eh Jackson," Jimmy titters to himself on the touchline as Jack picks the ball out of the net and launches it back to the centre circle for the demoralised bibs to restart the game.

Madness is not essential but it helps if there is a degree of insanity in the family to play the game.

At least today the reserves are comprised of flesh and blood and not a flimsy fabric from Gunn and Moore Sports. And therein lies another problem because unlike the bibs, apprentices, younger pros and older discarded ones not only move appreciably quicker but they also possess emotions, harbouring grudges that can surface with devastating effect in an unguarded moment. The unguarded part is more often than not the first team player who is not wearing shin pads or prepares for a tackle in the belief that his opponent is actually working for the same club and towards the same goal. Whereas in fact, it is a hotbed of festering disaffection with his lot in life that is approaching on the blind side. A young apprentice hoping to impress with his aggression or an old lag intent on damage, sick and tired of being selected for the 'Stands Team' every Saturday. "That won't pay the mortgage, Macca," on a regular basis, Brindley reminds those who are paying one. He is right. If you are not on the park, sub or in the stands as travelling first reserve, you earn only that handsome reserve bonus. £2 for a win and £1 for a draw. Members of the Stands Team gather only splinters in their backsides not win bonuses. And Brindley would be prepared to kick his granny into Row B for the chance to earn the money. Broken ankle or not.

Diary of a Football Nobody

Since I am in the reserves now, I don't take liberties with the likes of Brindley or Stubbo or Bradd. Everyone knows that. There are some players the Stiffs can kick lumps out of in practice matches; and there are some you can't. Stevie Newell, an apprentice right winger with a malleable body swerve that was positively rock rigid compared with his spine, discovered the true meaning of that simple doctrine the hard way.

The yellow streak painted down his backbone was long and wide but Stevie, local lad made good, thought he was safe in training games. Thus his 16-year-old frame found it amusing to turn big Bob Worthington this way and that during the course of a game. In short, he made him look a complete ass but when Brindley and Needham began to enjoy his torture, the normally placid Bob snapped. "Whoosh," and the trusty left foot landed the fragile Stevie Newell on the dirt track by the County Road Stand after half an hour of this particular dress rehearsal.

Enough had been enough and from that day henceforth, an unwritten truce had been agreed. You can have ten minutes making me look an utter pratt Stevie, but come near me again and you will face the consequences. Little Stevie obeyed the code, switching to the left wing where of course he came up against Brindley so basically he didn't get another kick and if he did, it was a one-touch back inside. The flamboyant, talented tormentor of the high and mighty stayed at home for the rest of the morning. Once, he transgressed and broke the treaty. The entire pitch went almost silent after he had skinned Bob inside and out on a sunny morning at Meadow Lane. Like

the school assembly awaiting the inevitable 'thwack' of the cane administered by Sir on an unruly and disobedient pupil, Bob's left boot was unerring in finding its intended target and wielding its punishment "I did warn you, Stevie son," Bob announced to a bemused and battered apprentice in right wing sorcery lying in a crumpled heap on the touchline. If Stevie wasn't sure that he had overstepped the mark, he knew now.

Even if Bob was not playing, the mental scars remained for Stevie. One morning he was not selected for the reserves so was chosen to run the line. He immersed himself in his role, joyously removed from the heat of battle and the potential for pain even if Stubbo threatened to give him a bloody good hiding when he refused to raise his flag for an obvious offside that allowed Vint to make it 1-0 to us.

Apart from the gaffer, the most obvious target for revenge is Masson. But he is quick and cunning and few get a sniff of blood. Only Sammy Dyer, who clatters people for fun, gets close. Once, too close for comfort, he caught him so well that the 'wee fellow' retired hurt, in a furious sulk, to the dressing room. This morning, though, it is a fairly dull affair. The first team lose 2-0 but report no injuries before Fulham tomorrow night.

Wednesday, August 28

Grimsby Reserves beaten 3-1 at Meadow Lane. Scored, 25 yarder that the goalkeeper should have saved but he was a young trialist. At this level you expect that sort of thing. First team hammered 3-0 at Craven Cottage. Smithy,

Collier and myself relaxed with a few beers in the TBI then the Flying Horse before engaging in the culinary delights offered by Arkwright Street. The Star of India suffices with a Spanish omelette and chips; Smithy decides on something more exotic and walking home is caught short. Dirty little sod that he is, he nips over an unsuspecting resident's wall and dumps his load in the backyard. His underpants serve as toilet paper which he then throws into the adjacent yard of the neighbour. And he wonders why he is exiled to his own little bath after training.

Tuesday, September 3

A tactical debriefing today. Put the ball away and let's get back to basics - at least for an hour anyway. "Everyone get changed and meet in the first team dressing room at 10.15," Ronnie announces to those of us down in the away team dressing room. That means the entire squad, 22 pros, six apprentices and Jack squeezed around the benches above which just 12 black and white shirts are hung up on a Saturday afternoon. Pedro is told to get the green board and tin can out of the cupboard in Jack's room. He places it in the middle of the room on the table across which boots, socks, tie-ups and gum packets are normally strewn. It is pristine today with only the board, stiff wood and mapped out in the shape of a football pitch, and the tin can on top.

A certain amount of anticipation hovers in the air. Publicly, Jimmy is seldom critical of his players; in fact publicly he seldom gives very much away to the media. "Good morning Jimmy," Terry Bowles, the local reporter

from the Post, offered by way of engaging Jimmy in conversation after training. "Nothing good about it if you're dead, eh," and another variation on a theme of his, another priceless gem went unquoted to the Nottingham public.

Behind closed doors he can be scathing, though, and the prospect of humiliation in front of your peers is a chilling one. 10.17 and the interior swing doors hurtle back and Jimmy walks in with Ronnie by his side; like the Wing Co and one of his aides sweeping into a secret bunker to convey the latest mission instructions. Jimmy has shed his tracksuit bottoms. Clad in outsize black shorts and with black socks rolled up to just below the knee, this is the business suit attire. We are in for a half hour at least.

The lecture cannot begin without the contents of the tin can. It is upside down with a plastic top seal holding them in. The top is loose, however, deliberately left that way by Pedro and 22 Corona lemonade bottle tops cascade all over the table and floor.

"Jesus, Ronnie, eh," Jimmy is laughing uncontrollably, snorting at intervals. It is a ritual perpetrated by Pedro. Occasionally the gaffer will spot it and "tut, tut" in the direction of Pedro or play along with the prank. Today he appears in good spirits.

Jack rises from his seat and helps him set up the 11 blue and yellow bottle tops in their appropriate formation. There follows a frantic quarter of an hour as Jimmy whooshes and whizzes the bottle tops at a variety of angles around the board. "And it doesn't do any harm to cleak this little fellow, eh," he explains, deftly ejecting

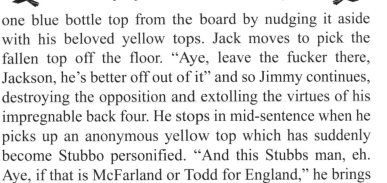

one blue bottle top from the board by nudging it aside with his beloved yellow tops. Jack moves to pick the fallen top off the floor. "Aye, leave the fucker there, Jackson, he's better off out of it" and so Jimmy continues, destroying the opposition and extolling the virtues of his impregnable back four. He stops in mid-sentence when he picks up an anonymous yellow top which has suddenly become Stubbo personified. "And this Stubbs man, eh. Aye, if that is McFarland or Todd for England," he brings two blue tops up against the yellow top, strategically positioned in the centre of defence on his own 18-yard box. "Aye, this is Brian, eh," and he brings another yellow top, probably David Needham, from nearby and erects a double decker bottle top. "Christ he's a giant, eh. If only you were Scottish, Brian, eh," and he giggles at the thought safe in the knowledge that he indeed has a giant at the back that other clubs envy.

Eventually, with bottle tops in disarray, the game is over. It is 11.10. Time for the squadron to scramble and head for the Hill to test the theory in practice match 412.

Watched Forest reserves in drab 1-1 draw at City Ground in the evening. Only highlight was Steve Baines being sent off. Ronnie was there; so was Brian Clough. Brother Paul has a theory of his sacking from Leeds United, in that they deliberately hired him to fire him and so eradicate the opposition, vindicating the FA's choice to choose Revie as England manager and not the people's choice. But then like my granddad, Paul doesn't believe the Americans sent a man to the Moon in 1969 or since, either. All done at Disney, he reckons.

Monday, September 9

Ran into an old Fairham school teacher, who said there had been talk in the headmaster's office of me packing in football. A conversation with Brian Bates, my old mentor, had sparked the rumour. Richard Nixon escapes scot free with a pardon and so endeth the great Watercloset scandal.

Friday, September 13

Flash Carter has been named substitute for the first team at Norwich City tomorrow. Most of us think it is a joke because at York City last week he didn't try a leg for the reserves. He has the knack of disappearing like the Pimpernel on wet and windy nights during North Midlands League games away from Meadow Lane. Get him on his home patch, though, and he is prone to turn it on for his appreciative audience. His talent is not in doubt but his commitment to the team ethic is. Still, Jimmy has decided he will give him more variety at Carrow Road while the reserves travel to Roker Park. Playing centre half again with instructions to go and win the ball in the air.

Saturday, September 14

Lost 1-0 to Sunderland but should have won. Felt genuine progress at the back. Sammy was encouraging throughout, tried to motivate everyone. Ronnie was pleased too. Something wrong somewhere, surely. The first team got a tonking at Norwich, 3-0. Met up with most of them in the TBI. There is the usual hardy core of supporters who regularly travel to away games and the Golden Girls, Amazing Grace and the women who aspire to read the graffiti underneath the arches of Trent Bridge. Probey is spotted down the 99 later, ducking and diving among the ruck and a star has been born in the ranks: Scanlon, Scan the Man Super Scan, who frequently scores spectacular goals in the reserves, has been elevated to the first team on the pitch and the dance floor.

Thursday, September 19

The precocious children of Greenholme School occupy an idle afternoon as Nixo and myself discuss his desperate desire to move on to Peterborough United. Even though they are in the Third Division he reckons he will be on the same money and net a couple of grand if Jimmy lets him go. The fathers of the precocious children of Greenholme School come to watch the game. "Pass it to Anthony" one of them urges. Slightly more refined than the "Give it to our Kev," heard on touchlines at Clifton Estate from dads hoping their prodigy will fill a vicarious void left by their own inabilities. Even so, the sentiment of human nature and the ambition for their son to succeed is no different regardless of the class divide. Where the similarity ends is when the mothers of the precocious children of Greenholme School come to collect their charges. Nixo will miss that Tuesday and Thursday afternoon interlude. Porridge illuminates a dull, sombre evening.

Friday, September 20

Jimmy has me in his office after training with Ronnie, his faithful lieutenant, by his side. He is unhappy with me living with Collier at Bingham; it is not a homophobic reaction, he clearly believes he is a bad influence. On this occasion, he has got his wires crossed and Ronnie has to point out that Collier is now in digs. Jimmy is in a reasonable mood. He wants to know why I've always got my head down and he tells me to shave off my beard which has reached Captain Birdseye proportions. He can fuck off.

Brindley has organised a work's outing in the afternoon, a trip to Birmingham to pick up eight cars for a chap in the motor trade. He has promised us a fiver each - IF we deliver the cars back safely. The married lads, Arthur, Eric Mac, Sammy, the Bolt and Vint, are all in for the extra money and the crack. Braddy, too. A watering hole stop on the way over at Ashby-de-la-Zouch then we hurtle back to the Halfway Garage at Bunny in convoy. Sammy desperately wanted to take the MGB back but Billy overruled him. I got a 1750 Maxi, the Vint a Marina and we nearly crashed the lot when he made an unexpected U-turn on the A-38. Headline: County game called off after eight die at the wheels of British Leyland cars. In the event Sammy breaks down in his Maxi after giving it more right boot and clog than he normally reserves for his opposite numbers in central midfield. Back at Bunny; the money is dished out, cash, by Brindley then most of it drunk across the road in the Rancliffe Arms.

98

BILLY BRINDLEY:

On both sides of the River Trent, Billy always gave 100 per cent, whether it was in pursuit of 'fancy dan' left wingers or that last pint of lager before closing time. Occasionally, but not very often, both could be elusive and frustrating in equal measure.

Steak...Diana Ross

Monday, September 23

Nixo has signed for Peterborough. He leaves Greenholme and me with Billy's egg round behind. Must have been a wrench.

Wednesday, September 25

'Super Scan' they were chanting at the first team game at Meadow Lane last night. Scanny scored in a 1-1 draw with the Orient. As always, those not selected are supposed to turn up for the match but I had arranged to meet Paul for a few pints over at Newark. It's not so bad for an evening match. Most of the lads pop into the dressing room and soak up a bit of the atmosphere before kick off. You want to be part of it, you want to be sitting there in shorts, socks and boots, on the receiving end of a perfunctory massage from Jackson. In one corner, Masson insists on a personal touch in jovial mood to warm him up; Brindley gets the legs warm with a few on the spot bursts. For The Claw, it is two tubes of Deep Heat, all over his body, rubbed in fervently between the undergrowth he calls back hair. "Don't shake it dry when you go for a piss," Brindley reminds him, unnecessary advice for the veteran. But even the old pros can forget. Gerry Gow, twenty minutes into the game against Bristol City after he has given me the runaround from kick off. "Not to worry, son, my bollocks have been on fire since I rubbed Deep Heat into them. When it wears off, I'll slow down." He didn't.

The dressing room buzzes in preparation and the outcasts, attired in suits and kipper ties as a mark of respect, are told to leave the premises by Ronnie at around 7pm. The serious business is about to begin, working up to the gaffer's team talk and analysis before the 7.25 run down the tunnel. "All the best lads," the departing ensemble echo, not meaning a word of it. Last night, I meant it even less having a pint of bitter in the Fox at Kelham but I know I would not have been conspicuous by my absence. There are enough false well wishers to camouflage my absence and afterwards in the Centenary Bar, Super Scan would have been the main attraction.

Donnie reserves at Belle Vue tonight provides a suitable alternative. 4-0 up in the first five minutes and half the team hadn't even had a touch. A late stop at Bawtry to celebrate victory with a swift pint in the local pub followed by fish, chips and beans and a game of cards on the team coach. Clearly, we must thrash Doncaster Hopeless 5-2 more often.

Thursday, September 26

Transported Vance Wood and his kitchen sink to Birmingham University. A land of glorious opportunity for Vance on campus and later, when he qualifies to be a French teacher, his fantasies fulfilled of shagging an endless supply of sixth form virgins. Not a bad ambition. A good luck handshake, keep voting Labour mate, refuse to conform and don't let the bastards grind you down. Lost in Lichfield on the way home but escaped via

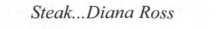

Steak...Diana Ross

Tamworth for an early pint in the Salutation in town, packed with the Sneinton Chapter of the Nottingham Hell's Angels and their molls. There has to be a better way than this, surely.

Friday, September 27

He may have his faults but when Ronnie Fenton goes into bollocking mode, it's best to break out the tin helmets. Saw a different side to him this morning - something much more admirable. Geoff Collier, who has been bemoaning his ill luck and blaming the world and his dog for it, began it. In fairness to him, he scored a huge amount of goals for the reserves last season without getting a genuine shot at the first team. When he was selected the match was called off and Braddy, who was injured, regained fitness and, quite rightly, was restored to the centre forward position. But that's football. I feel for him, even though we couldn't see eye to eye when we lived at Bingham. That small rift healed long ago but he joined the professional ranks at the same time as me and he has found it harder to adapt to the daily grind and rigours of training and the full-time game. Today, feeling more than a little sorry for himself, he lashed out at young Benjy during an eight-a-side on a hockey pitch up the Hill, a regular and enjoyable diversion for the reserve rabble on Friday mornings while the first team remain at Meadow Lane for a 'chuke up' or five-a-side with Jimmy.

Ronnie, who joins in, is incensed with Collier for what he says is a coward's way of exacting revenge. It is one of the unwritten laws of the game that you don't pick on an apprentice, no matter the circumstances.

Ronnie, five foot eight of raw-boned rage, motions towards Collier, 6ft 4in and pretty pissed off with the world in general. It stops short of physical contact; Ronnie is seething but knows he would be overstepping the line if he initiated a fisticuffs; a handbags at four o'clock it would not have been, however. Thereafter Ronnie gives everyone a piece of his mind - an enlightening but unpleasant experience. Flash comes off the worst, the sort of fancy dan Ronnie can't abide, telling him he needs a 'wet nurse' to survive in life, before rapidly hurtling on to his next victim. Back at Meadow Lane, Collier storms off and misses the weights session in Peter's potting shed beneath the stands. He has asked for his cards and is going home.

Saturday, September 28

Travelled as 13th man to Burnden Park today. No collar or tie and beard still intact. The usual pre-match at The George, then sat with directors and the Golden Girls in the posh box at Bolton. Strange contrast but both parties are fairly well acquainted with the players' private affairs and parts. 1-1 draw.

Monday, September 30

It appears a bloke just can't nod off in his own car without incident. Startled by water being poured carefully through the top of the driver's window onto

my head in an attempt to wake me from my alcohol-induced sleep. Concerned family, friends and half of Listowel Crescent are awaiting the outcome of International Rescue's latest escapade that included rocking the Fiat violently and hammering on the roof, all to no avail. Mission accomplished by 11.45pm under the street lights of No.19. The culmination of a severe session with Collier, a kind of wake for the big man that began in the Flying Horse and all but ended in a bed of nettles when I succumbed to the call of nature somewhere in a ditch near Ruddington.

Tuesday, October 1

The expected mouth like the bottom of a parrot's cage arrived in the morning. However, no headache and scored two in training for the reserves and the gaffer is pleased. There is a God, perhaps. An entertaining evening in the Salutation, graced by George Melly who is in town performing. Back home, John Conteh is champion of the world and Badger on The Old Grey Whistle Test make it a slightly less frantic conclusion to the night than the previous one.

Wednesday, October 2

Played left back at Valley Parade for the reserves; a bleak setting and night for a game of football. We had to walk a million miles from the dressing rooms to the pitch in the doom and gloom before emerging down a long concrete ramp greased with torrential rain. There

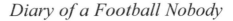

was more chance of injury on that perilous journey to and from the dressing rooms than on the pitch. Ces Pod, veteran of a million games for Bradford City, played at the back. A true pro and a real gentleman on the pitch, his conduct was an example to us all. Probey's fault for one of the goals but by sticking at it we scraped a 2-2 draw with the last kick of the game. We had stopped for a pre-match at the Crown, Bawtry. A nice steak but no Jimmy to conjure up some of his famous culinary etiquette. Talking to other players at other clubs, it appears we are fortunate to be served steak before some reserve games; Halifax are lucky to have a bus and a Mars bar. Last season, having won the North Midlands League title, we were treated to a post match celebration after the final match at Middlesbrough, steak with all the trimmings, and an alcoholic drink. The apprentices reluctantly decided on shandies but the Bolt and Sammy, like schoolchildren allowed a taste of freedom, managed to throw down three pints before the pudding arrived. Ronnie was not best pleased.

Thursday, October 3

Training crap - but one compensation in the wage packet. £40 extra for the draw bonus at Bolton on Saturday. First bonus for some time. Will pay for service on car and a few singles I need to record for the cassette. The gaffer has told me that the beard must come off if I am selected for the first team. Bollocks to that.

Friday, October 4

A funeral taking place just around the corner for four young lads killed in a car crash on Saturday night. I remember coming home, along Queen's Drive and being slowed down by police because there had been a fatal accident. The wide road that runs alongside the winding River Trent and in front of the Power Station and where Clifton Colliery once stood is a notorious one for speeding cars overtaking. Mark Guyler, no more than three years older than me, was one of the passengers who was killed instantly. And I recalled idle days playing with him and enjoying his friendship at school and at his house. A horrible, wet, miserable day to mourn the dead and say goodbye to wasted lives.

Tuesday, October 8

"I'm not going to play that McBay at Manchester to sweep up at the back, eh Jackson." It's hard to reply to that sentiment, expressed by Jimmy during his team talk this morning. The right name would have been nice gaffer, but it is the thought that counts and at least I am in his mind for the game at Old Trafford on Saturday. It is going to be a biggy and a test of our ambitions this season. Met up with Viv Anderson and Peter Wells in the afternoon for a cheese toastie, the famous three from Fairham Comp who are the pride and joy of R J Thom, the headmaster. Collier rang from Blackpool. He's returned to Macclesfield, £300 plus £100 as signing-on fee with the chance of a further £100 on appearances. £25 per week, he's happy as a pig in shit, even more so when he finds a job.

Wednesday, October 9

Bus in from Clifton for the reserve game tonight. The car is knackered and having some bodywork done over at Newark. Beat Halifax 6-0 and scored. The game played at a canter, men against boys. Not the usual stroll where at three up, you decide to go through the paces. The incentive to perform is a chance of a trip to Old Trafford on Saturday and everyone wants a place on that particular team coach. On to 99 later where the more serious extra marital affairs of players both sides of the Trent are acted out. "They are in love with them," Brindley surveys the scene around the dance floor mockingly. "Bloody slags" the players call them although these are married women themselves stealing away on their "night out" for another furtive moment in the shadows of a riverside night club. Not for these romantics the arches of Trent Bridge, more regular day time assignations; when the spouses are away, the mice can play. And they do, but not that any of the married lads ever boast about it. The likes of Smithy will embellish a quick snog as a night of unbridled passion, with himself in the assertive and starring role, but that is acceptable as well as amusing. He is young and single; the equation is simple. In the married quarters of Notts County, the issues are anything but black and white.

The beard, referred to on local radio, before it developed a brain of its own and took over my face. As well as power cuts and fuel shortages, note that combs and hairbrushes were rationed during the Great Crimpers' Strike of 1974.

108

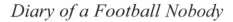
Thursday, October 10

The colour red is prominent in thoughts today (shocking lack of originality due to lack of time, line originally used February 28). May be travelling to Old Trafford to play United. Voted Labour, of course, in a hurry and dashed off to take charge of Greenholme school children. Furthering the socialist cause is not the priority in their households tonight, to be sure.

Friday, October 11

Labour 1, Greenholme School 0. Returned with a working majority of three. Will wear the no.12 shirt as substitute in Manchester. McBay will be there, just in case we sneak a lead and need to protect it with extra men back. The red revolution has begun! Celebrated with a night in watching Kung-Fu and M.A.S.H.

Saturday, October 12

"And on Match of the Day tonight, David McVay will be the one with the beard," was how Colin Slater, the Radio Nottingham commentator, described the team line-ups to radio listeners. In fact, they had no need to worry. Jimmy urged me to have a quick 'chuke up' shortly before half time but a few eyebrow stretches and feeble limbering up exercises by the touchline, carefully chosen away from the yelling yobs of the Stretford End, was as close as I got to the action. Managed to stand in the middle before kick off, where granddad ate his sandwiches as the bombs dropped on Manchester and the docks during the war. I can at least tell him that. All the stars were there for United: Pearson, Greenhoff, McIlroy, Buchan, familiar faces to football fans and players. An interpreter was required for Tommy Docherty, the manager, and Jimmy vying for the most indecipherable and obnoxious Scottish accent in the dug outs. The meaning, though, was lost on none of the players on the park. We lost a fast and furious game 1-0 but were far from disgraced. Flash was outstanding in typically fleeting moments but the luck held for United.

The novelty of free drinks in the Players' Bar later proved a stimulating talking point for us all and another highlight that Match of the Day cameras failed to record.

On the way up Jimmy had a quiet word. I would be fined a week's wages if I didn't shave the beard off. "I don't want you representing me like that, eh." "Yes boss."

So much for that little rebellion then McVay. Won't crush my independence, will they? The prospect of being £25 out of pocket next week is a most persuasive weapon in the revolutionary war.

Thursday, October 24

The beard has been suitably trimmed but the going is soft to heavy at Colwick Park, the racecourse being one of several training venues when the sporting needs of the students of Trent Polytechnic hold sway over Notts County's and force us to find an alternative. The ground near Burton Joyce, adjacent to the pig farm and the sewage works, is another. If the doggies don't finish you off, the smell will when the wind is blowing in the wrong direction. The pitches at Colwick, at the far end of the race track in front of the Hall, are more accustomed to amateur park players with hangovers, stale Park Drive breath and a lack of co-ordination between brain and limbs on Sunday mornings. In general, on a tedious, tactic morning, we provide reasonable substitutes. Jimmy wants to stage an attack on his back nine, the goalkeeper, his back four and midfield four before the game at Bristol City on Saturday. That means the four stooges, the Bolt, me, Sammy and Vint must impersonate the City front two and two midfield suppliers. That means me and Sammy standing on the halfway line of a grotty, undulating park pitch with the freezing rain teeming down, the sweat top shipping water like one of those old lace footballs, trying to find the Bolt, a centre half, and the Vint, nicknamed the Lincolnshire poacher by the local rag because he scores goals and was born in Boston. For a full hour the charade is played out. The first team midfield dutifully closes down me and Sammy but allows us, now and again, to make a telling pass to feet, galvanising the central defenders Stubbo and Needham to close down what passes for Bristol City's front two. Vint, keen to impress, occasionally eludes Stubbo or Neddy; the Bolt is more concerned when next he will experience the pleasures of nicotine.

The night shift production line at British Leyland probably experience greater job satisfaction and a more stimulating hour adjusting windscreen wipers on Morris Marinas as they idle along the conveyor belt.

There is a brief respite when Jimmy blows his whistle and intervenes for the umpteenth time. "David, David, fucking Jesus Christ," he walks towards Neddy who would be arrested if he moved any closer to Vint's backside. "David, get tight, tighter son." And Neddy obeys. "How fucking tight is tight, eh David," Jimmy shouts as he walks off towards the touchline. "Jack Dunnett's wallet, boss?" replies Neddy but the joke is lost on Jimmy in the winds whipping around the racecourse.

An afternoon at the snooker hall near the Theatre Royal and a Monty Python without mirth in the evening completed a worthless, tedious and ultimately futile day.

Friday, October 25

Flu jabs in the morning to see us through winter followed by shuttle runs after training with the first team departing for Bristol. The shuttles take place in the sand pit, three sets of doggies, short and sharp sprints, twisting and turning in the stamina-sapping sand.

Under the Mural at the Playhouse Bar with resident pseuds in attendance passed the night away. The concept is either a showcase for young and upcoming talent or the opportunity to drink for an extra hour after the 10.30pm closure, depending on your point of view.

Thursday, October 31

A fume-filled drive to Wilford Tip this morning in the Bolt's 1971 Vauxhall VXW/90. The green machine fuelled by tobacco. The wind is howling and we warm up by forming two circles and working the goalkeepers in the middle, shooting from all angles. As we clear the Bolt's smoke out of our hair, a green Morris Minor trundles into the car park. Frank, our staunch and loyal supporter from West Bridgford, emerges from the driving seat. It is a sprightly movement for someone of pensionable age. Braddy, who lives near to him, reckons Frank must be in his early 70s. Pristinely attired in three-quarter length dog-toothed coat and matching hat, Frank watches from a respectable distance as the warm-up continues. In the prevailing conditions it is not long before Stubbo launches one into the stratosphere, the Mitre ball heading off towards Gamston spurred on by a gust of wind. Frank seizes the moment, holds onto his hat and dashes off at a fair clip to retrieve the errant ball. Five minutes later he has returned with his trophy, dropping it from his hands and volleying it in the direction of Jimmy. "Bloody hell Frank, can't you make it a bit quicker next time," Braddy smiles earnestly in talking to Frank, who exchanges conversation with several players about their form and the team's poor showing of late during the morning. Later, he is perched by the side of Eric Mac's goal for the practice match, a dangerous position given the first team's appalling efforts to hit the target of late. "Catch it Frank," Brindley shouts as another effort fizzes beyond the post leaving Frank diving for cover in slapstick mode. "Jesus Frank, you must do better than that, eh son," Jimmy joins in the jollities. And Frank, one of our inner circle, is loving every minute.

Steak...Diana Ross

Friday, November 1

The writing has been on the wall for some of the first team over the past few weeks. I am recalled to the side at home to Hull City tomorrow. The trip to Manchester was a hint from the gaffer and a couple of steady performances in the reserves helped although the disappearing hair-off-the-face act probably swung the issue. "You are ready for it now, son," Jimmy told me. Ronnie was more blunt, saying that I hadn't earned the right to play in the first team for so long last season but had to learn my trade in the reserves before I could be restored. If he had his way, I wouldn't be in the bloody A team. Deliver a few of Brindley's eggs to his customers in the afternoon and prepare nervously for battle with a grapefruit juice and lemonade in the Admiral Rodney at Wollaton and the company of several old friends.

Saturday, November 2

Nerves and butterflies while watching Football Focus previews on Grandstand. It is quite strange to be part of the first team again. You become familiar with reserve team routines, the lack of genuine pressure and the uninhibited approach to games. The crowds, the atmosphere and tension of first team matches does not infiltrate until you have parked up at the ground. We are not the best supported side in the division by any stretch but 12,000 inside Meadow Lane can generate a reasonable atmosphere. The Stands Team enter and usher in their insincerity. "Good luck Macca," only the name has

114

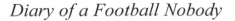

changed, the sentiment hasn't. The thespian equivalent of break a leg would be more appropriate in the literal sense in our profession.

The pace and movement at this higher level takes your breath away after a long spell in the stiffs. On the right side of midfield, the traffic is busy; Hull, though, are not the most inventive side and allow the opposition time and space to consider options. Masson is in good form. Again. After a solid if unexceptional start I am beginning to get the feel and tempo of the Second Division again. Fitness is not a problem, sharpness of thought and feet are initially. An hour has passed and we are coasting, four up and onto our biggest win of the season, 5-0. 65th minute; a loose ball on the right by the County Road Stand. A nick around the left back and suddenly we have lift off, clattering to earth after an innocuous tackle that didn't hurt in the slightest. So much pain when I put weight on the left ankle, though, that I am forced to retire hurt. The ankle is the size of a cricket ball and Jack tells me to report on Monday morning when the swelling has receded. "No alcohol, no driving and complete rest until then David." Fat chance. Drinks in the Flying Horse with the Bolt and Smithy and on to party at Gedling.

Monday, November 4

There is something about injuries that attracts crowds with a lust for blood and gore only matched by Coliseum fans in ancient Rome or foxhunting toffs. The entire squad invade the limited space of Jack's treatment room this morning. "Come on, Billy, you don't need anything

in here you bloody man," Jack urges Brindley to leave his room as he sneaks a look at my inflated ankle. "It'll be a few weeks with that my son," he opines with a considered and knowing look. "No sort of tackle at all, was it Macca." Thanks Billy. Does that mean I'm as soft as grease or what. After the plebs have had their say, Jimmy makes his compulsory visit to the stricken peasant, the surgeon pronouncing judgement on his rounds. Nixo once related the story of his injury when Jimmy came in prodding and probing his fingers and thumbs into his right ankle with all the compassion of the Boston Strangler. "How does that feel, Jon?" he asked with Jack in attendance. "Not too bad boss." The grip tightens and the ankle is tilted to an awkward angle. "Canya feel that son?" "No boss." "Aye, that's a bad one all right, Jon. Jack, get some hot and cold [water] on this, eh." Of course, as Nixo explained, he didn't have the heart to tell him he'd been touching up the wrong ankle.

He is spot on this morning, though, and I nearly hit the roof before Jimmy's tale of the worst ankle injury in the world re-emerges. Jack ferries me to the General Hospital in the afternoon. After an hour's wait in X-ray, we are told there is serious ankle ligament damage and a plaster is required, fitted under anaesthetic. By four o'clock, Jack takes me home groggy and depressed.

Tuesday, November 5

Bonfire night party on crutches. The local paper reports that I shall be out for at least six weeks with a special brief to keep an eye on my weight. So why am I standing here

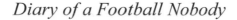

with a gin and tonic and sausage sarnie in my hand watching the Catherine Wheels rotating violently?

Tuesday, November 12

A week without a car and training; of limping and hopping on and off buses, in and out of public bars and glued to television. Softly, Softly, Z-Cars and documentary called Fat Man on the Beach about B.S. Johnson, poet and artist who committed suicide eight weeks after it was made, have been the highlights. Bought Unhalfbricking by Fairport and ELO's On The Third Day to lift the gloom. A new plaster fitted yesterday because the old one had cracked. Pain had been unbearable for the last few days but this plaster will not come off until December 2. And on Budget Day, the Government announce an 8-10 and half pence increase in petrol. Marvellous.

Thursday, November 14

Training re-commences in Peter's potting shed. Multi-gym circuits monitored by Jack with irritating Smithy interruptions. He's got some girl into trouble and is in a mess so, despite my frustrations at lack of mobility, his sense of humour can be tolerated this morning. A bath at my home with plaster balanced on the side and Jimmy asking how it's going son. "Not bad boss," and it's good to be back in the routine which began when Brindley gave me a lift in and immediately set off to deliver eggs to the Queen's in Beeston. Ah, those good old days, Billy . . .

Saturday, November 16

Illness and disability brings out the best in those who are not afflicted. One half decent game against Hull City and a bad injury and suddenly all the supporters in the Centenary Bar wish me well and insist that the first team needs me. Bollocks. Watched with the Stands Team at Meadow Lane as Scanny scores a hat trick in less than three minutes. Super Scan has really arrived although a cracker by Eric Potts rescues a point for Sheffield Wednesday in a 3-3 draw. Great entertainment but Jimmy is flat later. After a superb win at 'Aston Vanilla' the previous week he had expected another two points to climb up the table. Oh! What a Lovely War at the Playhouse on Saturday night keeps me off my plaster and off the booze.

Friday, November 22

A meaningless day of aimless ambition topped off with news reports of IRA bomb outrages in Birmingham pubs and thoughts of granddad in hospital, tubes in his mouth and neck and disfigured face from operation to remove cancerous cells from his shoulder. Nick Drake and restless sleep is calling.

Thursday, November 28

Collier rang. He is scoring in equal abundance on and off the park, one for Macclesfield against Boston United last Saturday and countless more - give or take the odd five

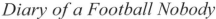 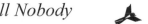

for embellishment - in Blackpool's clubs and bars. Have arranged to see him next weekend when the plaster is off and the first team are at Bloomfield Road. Good weights session then onto Plumptre Arms, the team's local in The Meadows just a stone's throw across the London Road from Meadow Lane. Darts and a game of bar skittles washed down by several pints of lager negates all the hard work of the morning but makes me feel much more optimistic about the future.

Saturday, November 30

Pedro makes his home debut with an own goal but plays well and gets a sympathetic vote of approval from the crowd. Millwall are beaten 2-1, all the goals coming in the first 10 minutes. Good result after last week's thrashing at Sunderland. A glorious interlude when Masson was chased by Arthur all over the pitch, the latter trying to exact revenge for another undeserved rollicking that broke the camel's back.

There is also the welcome, almost compulsory, intervention of Ronnie Chapman near the corner of the Meadow Lane stand. When the ball drifts out of play by that touchline, dear old Ronnie leaps over the low wall and iron gate that opens for the ambulances; a quick shimmy and a feint of his shoulders and he returns the wayward pass with interest to the nearest player trying to retrieve the loose ball. "Just like Tommy Lawton," he tells us when Smithy, Pedro and Benjy are walking in the Victoria Shopping Centre. It is a regular haunt for Ronnie, nipping into the Central Market café for a cup of tea and joining us or Brindley or any passing player to discuss the meaning of life and, more importantly, the team of frogs he trains at home. For long periods, Ronnie is lucid and knowledgeable about County's current form and that of the individual players, even if he calls them Les Gradd and Bob Skervington, but when the grasp on reality slips, it reveals a personality more than a couple of tadpoles short of a full pond. "Taught them any new tricks lately," we ask him because daily he trains each individual frog. "Coming along nicely, lads," Ronnie replies, slightly stuttering and breaking off with a sporadic twitch and Lawtonesque drop of the shoulder. "Ball control is bloody brilliant. Especially Stubbo. Hey, Stubbo, he takes no prisoners," and Ronnie rises to head another raking high cross to safety. On bad days, the thought of a tiny amphibian named after me hopping in spectacular fashion at Meadow Lane in a parallel universe is appealing. Wonder what frog heaven is like?

Monday, December 2

A month on and the man in the iron cast is free. Two and half hours at hospital but worth the wait. "Walk to Get Fit" is the headline in the Post. Sounds about my pace.

Thursday, December 5

Proceeding across the Victoria Embankment at 30mph (speed limit 20mph) when stopped by traffic policeman on motor bike. Men clad in leather always reminds me of

an unhealthy Emma Peel complex but at least he knew Brindley and let me off - after the grovelometer went off the scale.

Saturday, December 7

The Golden Mile, Golden Girls, Golden Goals, in fact anything that glistens beckons this weekend. The Claw requires someone to drive his green mini van to Blackpool so he can stay the weekend and Collier wants some of his old boots and training gear taken to Blackpool. In return he has promised a golden weekend. Halfway over the Pennines in the most uncomfortable car in the world that needs a man blessed with the brains of a rocket scientist and the brawn of Geoff Capes to change gear, I begin to regret making either promise of delivery. The wind is howling and in fourth gear, the fragile mini struggles to reach 35mph on the upgrade. Four and a half hours of torture continues at Bloomfield Road as the first team are soundly beaten 3-1. Jimmy spots me after the game and asks why I am here. "Just bringing Kevin's car for him boss." "Aye, and how are you getting home son," he asks, spotting Collier out of the corner of his eye. "Train boss," I could not tell a lie without offering further information. "Aye, you get on the team coach son and travel back with us." He never did like Collier nor his impact on me. Strangely, though I think he's an interfering bastard, I was quite pleased to get home and have an early Saturday night with every bone aching from the back-bending journey in The Claw's sardine can. Watched in disbelief as Ali lost his temper, cool and

seemingly his sense of reason when interviewed by Parkinson. We all thought the Butterfly was going to sting, severely, the intrepid Parky.

Thursday, December 12

Have been given the nod to start running in training this week but Ronnie and Jack have got the wrong end of the stick. I am not training for the bloody Olympics, just to get fit. Morning and afternoon, short and long stamina work punctuated by visits to the multi gym in the potting shed - Peter permitting that is. After this morning, the fourth consecutive day of pre-season training and a trip to watch the reserves hammer York City at a bare and bitter Bootham Crescent last night, I am knackered. There is some good news. Masson has departed to Queen's Park Rangers for £100,000, the deal between Jolly Jack and his chairman buddy Gregory at Loftus Road. "What a blow to morale," Brindley lamented in mocking tones this morning. In the absence of the wee fellow, hilarity breaks out in the dressing room. Even apprentices polish and deliver boots to the pros with a spring in their step. Even so, there is a distinct nervous twitch in the air. Who will be the new captain? How will Jimmy cope without his 'jewel'? And who is going to take all our corners, free-kicks and throw-ins from now on? The nights are certainly drawing in. But not before Pedro, celebrating his first team status, can pop into Birdcage and spend his first win bonus on two pairs of trousers and a shirt. It is the sort of boutique, on Bridlesmith Gate just around the corner from Paul Smith's shop, that should carry a sign above its door declaring: "Fat Boys Need Not Inquire Within." It is a favourite for the young Forest set but it helps if you are like Viv, spider-like and more meat on a jockey's whip as Brindley would say. Once I tried to squeeze into a pair of fashionable and pricey trousers upstairs; the shop assistants, young lads like us all, were definitely stifling guffaws. "Just a touch on the tight side," one of them ventured with Pedro and Smithy nodding in agreement. I wasn't built for fashion.

Sunday, December 15

A bitterly cold morning on the track at Meadow Lane. Told to report for training because I have been given the green light to start kicking a ball tomorrow - a month and a half after that bloody nothing challenge. Yes, Billy, I know. No sort of tackle at all, son. Scanny and Ray, who are injured, join me and Jack for a slight chuke up. Jack's brilliant. He may have his weaknesses as a bit of a 'yes' man to Jimmy but he is so genuine and supportive. He lets Scanny and Ray go and have a bath after their exertions then gets me running up and down the terraces of the County Road Stand, telling me the old stories of 20 mile runs in pre-season when he first came here as trainer nearly 20 years ago. There's also the one about the cows stampeding and breaking loose from the adjacent slaughterhouse in the Cattle Market and disrupting training one morning. Not even Jack expects me to believe that one, surely? A good session and the pain is far less when I put full weight on the ankle. It will all be over by Christmas!

Monday, December 23

All I want for Christmas is a severe bollocking from Ronnie for not applying myself in training. Can't remember if I put it on Santa's list that I sent to the grotto earlier in the month but that's what I got anyway - a little early, too. Still, he had a point although I haven't felt right on this ankle since I began kicking last week. It was good of the gaffer to include me in the first team warm-ups straight away, the play and move sessions before training. It instills confidence - but there are some, like poor old Sammy, who must feel a little resentment. If the first team squad were all killed in a Munich-style disaster, Peter the groundsman and Albert the chief tea masher, would get their pick ahead of Sammy. Now I haven't kicked a ball for six weeks and played 65 minutes of a Second Division game all season and I am included in plans straight away. It must gnaw but Sammy, despite being hard as nails on the pitch, is gracious enough not to pass comment - at least not in my earshot. So stop the moaning and whingeing and get your mind right.

Wednesday, December 25

That festive message from HRH R Fenton has been received and is sinking in. Training around the track with six laps to finish. Felt good. Merry Christmas boss, a different one from last year on the eve of the game with Forest on Boxing Day. Jimmy took us all away to the Posthouse at Sandiacre at night which for me was more

Half-time at Meadow Lane and the perils of ignoring dugout
instructions regarding movement off the ball. After 45 minutes of
static apathy, rigor mortis has gripped this hapless victim. Inside the
home team dressing room survivors are offered Albert's sweet tea
and sympathy. A blow torch from a plumber's merchant in the
nearby Cattle Market has been requested.

125

an inconvenience that restricted festivities to two pints of beer with the turkey at home. For the married lads with children, however, it was a real pain. A year of ducking and diving for some of them, with frequent household disruptions and arguments ending with the husband having to leave the family on Christmas Day night. The divorce papers followed them out of the door, no doubt.

Saturday, December 28

Memories of a glorious summer, driving into the City Ground, are revived this afternoon. Only today, the weather is cold, the ankle is hurting on the clutch pedal and I will be in the Stands Team. Still, a brilliant 2-0 victory over the enemy. Flash and Braddy score the goals. For once, I am pleased the first team has won in my absence. Not only won, but won well and won without Masson. There cannot be a better way for the Notts supporters to end 1974. At Raleigh, Player's and the two big breweries, Shippos and Home Ales, and on factory floors and shops, the black and white fans will walk a little taller on Monday morning.

Wednesday, January 1, 1975

I did tell Deirdre, a lovely picture of innocence, when she wanted something from the car, not to use the ignition key. But at 2am in the morning, she probably forgot. Result: Stranded in Beeston at her friend's flat on New Year's Day, awake to Angie Baby on the radio and desperately trying to get a bus, taxi or camel into training for 10am. Failed miserably. Late. Jimmy is furious, despite me ringing in earlier. "Yeh, of course your ignition key broke in the door lock. On New Year's Eve, as well," Probey obligingly points out. True but lame excuses don't count. A week's wages are docked but a lunchtime revival, eight pints and bar skittles with Brindley, Pedro and Smithy in the Plummie Arms erase the memory cells. Happy New Year.

Friday, January 3

Six laps in 8m 15 secs around the track today. Haven't surpassed the 7m 31 secs achieved last season but seem to be getting there. Even so, there is another one of those unwritten rules that you don't push too hard otherwise it puts pressure on colleagues. Nixo and Neddy, partners in the six laps, six horse shoes and six halves, had perfected the art of the dead heat in acceptable time. Even though you run in opposite directions, it was virtually impossible to split the two of them when they crossed at the opposite ends of the halfway line. Rehearsals were not necessary - the understanding was as telepathic as Keegan and Toshack of Liverpool. Keegan, as Jimmy constantly reminds us, could have been a Notts player. "Aye, £35,000 for Keegan at Scunthorpe," he recalls. But it was Bill Shankly who took the risk. Deliver egg money to Brindley, the egg master, and then onto FA Cup third round win over Portsmouth at the Lane. Crisp, crackling Friday evening match. Even the Stands Team, fuelled by several pints of beer, is happy.

Monday, January 6

Whatever Happened to the Likely Lads didn't quite happen to me or my friends but there is a Terry in all of us which appeals to those who don't polish the Vauxhall Victor or date as faithfully as Bob. Resisted the temptation to pop out for a few pints after another brilliant episode, staged mainly in the public bar of their local. Brian Clough is the new manager of Forest; that defeat against us was the last chance for Allan Brown.

Tuesday, January 7

As much as you can run six laps in less than eight minutes every day of the week and lift a few weights under the disapproving eye of Peter Thompson, there is no substitute for matches to regain full fitness. A 5-0 stroll over Doncaster Reserves will not instantly make me a candidate for the first team on Saturday and on reflection a gentle return against one of the worst sides in the North Midlands League was perhaps for the best. Hit the post and bar and came close to scoring; the same applied at the 99 later in the evening. The cutting edge to my game, fairly blunt at the best of times, has all but disappeared.

Saturday, January 11

While I have bored just about everybody with the idea of packing it all in and going to college or the dogs, depending on the mood at the time, Eddie Cliff is actually doing something positive about his dilemma. He came from Burnley last season with Probey and the two of them were highly rated in the side Jimmy Adamson was building to be the team of the '70s until the roof caved in at Turf Moor. Eddie is one of the young married professionals who is an exception to the rule of infidelity. He seldom goes out on the town unless it is a compulsory attendance for a celebration. Since his transfer, though, his chances have been limited at right or left back. He told me that he was definitely going to make the break from Notts and full time football, possibly going into teaching. "I wish you well, eh, Eddie," as Jimmy might say but he hasn't played him since we lost 5-1 at home to Wednesday last season. Even Sammy would edge him out if the entire first and reserve team went down with the bubonic plague. But I admire his resolve to turn his back on the game, if he does have the courage to match his conviction. Meanwhile, secured a stack of comp tickets (the lads in the office usually oblige unless it is a shipping order) with one or two mates up from college with their girlfriends. Why they would want to impress them with an afternoon at Meadow Lane watching Notts against Blackpool remains a mystery, more so after a 0-0 draw. Jack took me to one side after the game and asked me where I was at 2.30pm. "At the ground Jack," which was the truth. Apparently they had been looking for me or Ray O'Brien to play because Pedro had reported sick before kick-off. Shit! Must have been too busy working out allocation in the ticket office!

Monday, January 20

Gloom and doom in the air on Monday morning after the first team suffered a bad 3-0 defeat at Millwall. A good time for fringe players to state their case and two goals for the reserves this morning have helped mine, I'm sure. The Claw can sense a recall, too, and prepares for practice matches with even more Deep Heat plastered on his extremities. The mud and slushy conditions that prevail up the Hill means overtime for the most vital cog in the Meadow Lane machine - the boiler room. The interior of the hallowed room, rooted along the corridor and splitting the two opposing dressing rooms with its door just before the tunnel where the players run out before the game, resembles a cross between a Heath Robinson contraption and the courtyard of a Meadows back-to-back, two-up, two-down on wash day. The three senior residents, Albert the tea man, sits and chuffs on his cigarettes while discussing the meaning of life with Clara, a vibrant West Indian lady with a booming laugh, and Maude, of Meadows origin and earthy humour. In the summer months, the training kit is hung outside on makeshift lines just about where one of Stubbo's better passes or clearances usually land, with Albert, basking beneath the mass of blue numbered towels, flimsy jock straps and shorts, shirts and socks, lapping up the sunshine while inhaling the incongruous mixture of glorious fresh air and Park Drive. In the depths of winter now, the occupants are restricted to the oppressive heat of the boiler room; steam is everywhere, rising up from Albert's kettle and huge tea pot; escaping from the iron where Maude is putting the finishing touches to tomorrow's shirts; and finally billowing up from the hot water in the wash tub where today's muddied kit is idling around in jerky revolutions. The constant clouds of tobacco smoke emanating from Albert's nub-end completes an almost impenetrable barrier of steam and smoke. One of the gaffer's more eccentric team talks in the vicinity and the hot air rising would take the roof off the Main Stand above. Although it is principally the domain of the three grafters, the apprentices are often in and out, stopping off for a quick cup of the several brews Albert mashes during the course of a day. Aside from his vital duties of making the tea, he also ensures the huge concrete baths in the home and away team dressing room are almost full and piping hot when we return from training or the pitch at full time on match days. A degree or two over or under the threshold is met with a partial soaking for Albert who retaliates with his stories of Bendigo and his own experiences of unarmed combat. On less labour intensive days, Maude, Clara and Albert will impersonate contestants in a balloon debate, each making a case for their particular philosophy or doctrine in order to avoid being ejected to oblivion, arguing with passing apprentices or Jack about every conceivable aspect of modern life. In general, Albert is in the Enoch Powell camp while Maude and Clara tend to favour any party that will neuter their respective husbands. Bawdy, lewd but great entertainment at the end of a dull morning. Smithy swears he and Pedro have both had Clara, from behind over the tumble drier of course. Occasionally Smithy still propositions her but judging

from the reaction, he was crap the first time or he is telling porkies. Again. The inherent warmth from its coal-fired stove also attracts the senior pros on a cold, dank day, a naughty refuge for the likes of Stubbo to grab a clandestine smoke with his feet warming near the open part of the boiler. It's a natural progression from a crafty drag behind the bike sheds. It might be a health hazard but Jolly Jack would be delighted to know the flammable material and naked fire was in such close proximity beneath all that tinder wood.

Stubbo is in there today, drawing on a cigarette, surrounded by frenzied tea mashing, ironing and scrubbing and apprentices flitting in and out of the scene with dirty boots in hand or carrying a bottle of milk or tray of tea for the gaffer and Ronnie to enjoy in their offices. Like Heath Robinson, the whole concept works - how, nobody is quite sure. Stubbo is fretting about the side's poor result on Saturday and his place in the team. It is of course, a smokescreen. The double Corona bottle top may not win many debates in the descending balloon but he will never be dropped overboard by the gaffer.

Tuesday, January 21

And now for something completely different. A wet and windy Tuesday night at Halifax and yet another 6-0 win. The ball was of no consequence to the eleven men and true from Yorkshire as they intended to prolong our visit to the region in the local infirmary by attempting to kick lumps out of anything that moves in a black and white striped shirt. It is not an unusual experience in the North

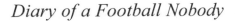

Midlands League - when you are so inferior in ability and class, there is only one last resort to turn to. Physical violence. However, there are too many old lags and young legs to be caught by a set of Yorkshire beef and pudding pies. The gaffer is delighted that we have stuck to our principles, the principles he cultivates, caressing and making love to the ball. For the Halifax contingent it was very much a knee trembler underneath the arches at Trent Bridge.

The drinks, and later the fish and chips, are on Jimmy in the Shay club house bar.

Saturday, January 25

FA Cup fourth round result from last night: QPR 3, Notts County 0. Wouldn't you know it was Masson the Marvellous. Saw highlights on Football Focus today and did look impressive. Even Arthur couldn't get close enough to land a telling blow on the wee man.

Saturday, February 8

After three months the gaffer has decided to take a chance on me again. A goal for the reserves and a 3-1 home defeat by Vanilla last week has clinched it. Jimmy called it a 'disgrace', privately of course. At least the disgrace was not me this time. In front of over 16,000 fans the lads had let the supporters down. The Claw returns, also, and it had to be Hull City, of course, but this time there is no fluke injury nor a 5-0 stroll. A desolate Boothferry Park that once vibrated to capacity crowds and Ken Wagstaff

Steak...Diana Ross

Come back, all is forgiven - well, not quite. We are talking football
fans here. After six weeks in plaster and a similar period of
rehabilitation, I have returned to stop the rot and bring to an end a
dismal sequence without winning - we lose 1-0.

134

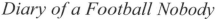 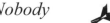

but now the only shudders, feeble at that, felt on the sparsely populated terraces are caused by the trains that wend their way around the corner of the huge ground. Even in the whirl of a mediocre Second Division match it is impossible to resist a moment of train spotting in such impoverished surroundings. Perhaps Stubbo was that man watching the trains goes by, jotting down the numbers on his notepad when he dropped a real clanger and tossed the game away. Could have won, should have won; lots of pressure, plenty of half chances but we just couldn't stick one away. An apology through the smoke of a hot bath and filter tip is not a substitute for the £40 draw bonus he has tossed away. "How tight is tight, eh Brian?" Without a bonus of any description for over a month, bloody tight. But then as a married man with children of his own he will appreciate that more than most.

Thursday, February 13

Jimmy is perplexed. Four straight defeats is the reason. "It becomes a habit, eh," he told the assembled troops this week. "Just like winning. The Shanklys and the Revies have that habit. But that's a good habit, eh," he snorts and laughs to himself as Brindley pinches the tight flesh on Probey's wrist, trying to make him wince or laugh in the face of this sombre logic. In an attempt to break the habit, Jimmy has dragged us to Leegreen, a teacher training college just north of the Arctic Circle in Matlock. Snow and freezing cold bedrooms greeted us last night and today we have stood around like penguins trying to keep warm in the Peak District. In the perishing cold, it is

img_1

9781903158371

difficult to focus on set-pieces and absorb tactical
information when the hands and feet are numb and the
testicles are receding rapidly, shrivelled and close to
dropping off. At night, Stubbo and Brindley head up an
escape committee and lead inmates to the nearest
watering hole, right out of the gates and a couple of
hundred yards down the road. With no searchlights and a
day off for the guard dogs, the escape is a success. In the
inclement weather, sport is best enjoyed indoors. Darts
and dommies contests and a card school are all quickly
arranged with several pints flowing from the tap room.
The gentle competition is interrupted by the distinctive
tones of Jimmy in deep conversation with Jack at the door
of the pub. Abandon pints, women and children last. Ten
grown men on hands and knees crawling out of the bar,
around to the snug via the toilets and heading out in the
bleak winter night back to the chilling reception of
Leegreen. Only Brindley and Stubbo accomplish it all
and could claim that at no time did their glasses of beer
once leave their hands. Nor did they spill a drop. True
pros in any crisis. Jimmy and Jack are left in splendid
isolation with two arrows still in the dartboard and the last
matchsticks in the cribbage board betraying a couple of
bar games that would never be completed.

Saturday, February 15

So there is method in Jimmy's madness. A 0-0 draw with
Sunderland at Meadow Lane stops the rot, brings a point
and more importantly, some extra cash. It could have
been double your money, though. Vint was a whisker

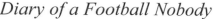 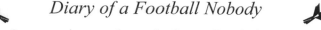

away from getting on the end of one. Sunderland, near the top of the table and heading for promotion behind Manchester United, are the sort of team that can play and also allow you to play. Dave Watson, at centre half, is solid and after a first half that went our way, we were glad of the point. The gaffer is beaming at the final whistle - he knew the habit had been broken and a clean sheet to boot.

Saturday, February 22

The sun shone on Hillsborough today; pity the fans were not there in abundance to appreciate the reflection on the famous ground. Vint scores the only goal of the game but we are far superior than a 1-0 win. The boss kisses us all after the game. The pressure of relegation that has crept up stealthily in recent weeks has been lifted - for now.

Sunday, March 2

Another night to remember at PFA dinner at the Hilton. Harold Wilson and Bernard Manning and the Vicar of Leeds deliver some great lines. Bacardi and Coke is even more expensive than last year. Alex Stepney, the one-save wonder, staggers in the main hall as if he's had £30 worth of them. The Playboy Club, courtesy of two gentleman of Chinese origin who signed us in, followed. All a bit jaded, seedy almost. Drinks in Soho and then in Brindley's room until wee small hours but somehow, it wasn't quite the same as last time.

137

Wednesday, March 5

Granddad gets worse. Asleep upstairs in the afternoon; shaking at night. Happy birthday.

Sunday, March 9

A day of school reports for the children of Greenholme School. Have been awarded the sheriff's badge for my display at Leyton Orient yesterday. A 1-0 win in the mud and sludge of Brisbane Road; ideal conditions for working off the Bacardi and beer from Thursday night's belated birthday binge. Scanny scored the goal but not enough to earn him eight out of ten in the Sunday People. At home games, it is a dash from the bath to the bar to find the man from the People and oil his joints with a couple of whiskies. It is only adding to the many he has been downing throughout the game. When some members of the Stands Team decide it is time to retire early to the Centenary Bar (quarter of an hour gone in the first half is a respectable length of time to make an exit, shouting loudly 'just popping to the loo'), the man from the People can occasionally be spotted at the bar, already on his third whisky chaser. Obviously the man from the People at Brisbane Road hit the top shelf before we even started. Even so, it is satisfying to get the star rating although there will be stick to follow in training. "He never even saw you, Macca" or it "Doesn't mean a thing". And they are absolutely right - until they get it.

Thursday, March 13

The kit is damp and soggy this morning. The tenuous strands of pipes and plaster that maintain efficiency in the boiler room have come apart. Players are grumpy; they require their boots polished pristine clean by apprentices otherwise the boot boys don't get the extra pound for making both the training boots and match day boots shine. Smithy, just turned pro, is as bad as anyone; the poacher turned gamekeeper who chastises the 'young apprentices' for not being diligent in their duties. "Just can't get the staff." He is joking but there is the distinctive tone of supremacy in his delivery. And who can blame him? He has served his time - scrubbing the floors and sinks, polishing the boots, painting the stands and fences with Jack in the summer and sweeping the terraces. Now these poor bastards are going to suffer.

Up the Hill the Trent Poly students (otherwise Polyfucks) have taken precedence for their training session and deprived us of a pitch. Jimmy spots a spare rugby one and we are on our way. Jack, playing in goal for the reserves, has difficulty with the height of the crossbar. "Come on Jackson, pick those out, eh." Jimmy is taunting him as Braddy chips him with ease from 40 yards. Jack, who has played in front of full houses at Highbury, Maine Road and Old Trafford before and after the war and reached heights in his career that Jimmy could never dream of, takes it all in his usual good heart. The tables are turned now, in the professional sense. Both men know their place. In the midst of the irreverent sparring, Flash and Scanny have their own squabble to resolve. A steady

flow of goals has persuaded Scanny that not only is he God's gift to women (in the 99 it is an argument that might stand up in court if the word 'women' is accepted in its loosest sense) but that he is also the most deadly predator to come out of Scotland since Rob Roy and Denis Law (this one will be thrown out by the jury). His hat trick in record time against Sheffield Wednesday and some crucial goals as well as a mate who sells dodgy second-hand cars from his lock-up in West Bridgford have been powerful allies in persuasion. Those of us who have marked him a hundred times a season in practice know he is a one-trick marvel; a shimmy and drop of the shoulder and instead of letting fly with his trusted left foot, he cuts inside and then outside before having a pop at goal. It foxes you the first dozen times; the next 20 you know what he is going to do but still can't prevent him from turning you; then you begin to get the gist of it, almost not bothering to shadow the first decoy strike before waiting, as for a bus, for the vehicle to break and spin round in rapid fashion.

It pisses Scanny off when the apprentices at centre half cotton on after a few minutes but in fairness to him, the opposition, when it matters most, haven't. "That's all that counts, son," Jimmy offers words of consolation when an exasperated fellow Jock feels harassed, losing possession on the edge of the penalty area after another telegraphed dummy ploy.

Flash Carter, his drinking buddy, has been a little miffed by the untoward attention afforded his room mate. But there is more; they have not been the best of mates on the field, either. Flash is dismayed that Scanny is becoming selfish on the ball (pot calls kettle black).

Scanny is hogging it as well as the limelight. He has taken over the mantle of the crowd's darling and up the Hill today the pair of them have a terrible tiff.

"They couldn't tackle a decent rice pudding," Needham mocks as the two square up and stop play to truly startled players. Jimmy, unimpressed with Trent Polyfucks, the rugby pitch and his two contestants, intervenes.

"You want to fucking fight, aye we'll have a fucking fight." And he marches off and tells the apprentices to mark out a square near the corner flag of the rugby pitch with yellow and red bibs. The game has stopped and the entire squad gather around. "Off you go," he yells at Scanny and Flash in the makeshift boxing ring but there is not the slightest hint of a shadow to box. Flash, inevitably, has seen the funny side; Scanny, intense and aggrieved, has not. Still, there is not a punch in sight and the dynamic duo is ordered to run back to Meadow Lane. Scanny sets off, angry and hurt, at 100 miles an hour while Flash jogs merrily behind by a good country mile. The game continues with Jimmy muttering: In the context of trench warfare there will be Brindley and Stubbs at the front line; Scanlon and Carter will be stamping forms and licking envelopes several miles behind at GHQ.

Saturday, March 22

Southampton is a long way to go for a 3-2 defeat to three shitty goals. Scanny gets two. Great! More grief from Rob Roy. Channon, who I am supposed to be marking,

never had it so easy. Several gin and tonics and cigars at Mr Miller's, Nottingham's newest and finest night club late on Saturday night, obliterate the memory of it all. Probey stays the distance but even in his Hopkirk white he cannot pull. Take him home, inebriated, to Cotgrave, before he annoys anyone else.

Friday, March 28

The car park between the Leen River, Iremonger Road (named after the giant goalkeeper who played for Notts in the 1920s) and the Cattle Market serves two useful purposes. It accommodates the cars of match day permit holders on Saturday and the players on Friday mornings; an ash-laden and confined surface for the first team squad to demonstrate the art of ball control. A treacherous and unreliable mixture of gravel and grit, it is nevertheless a great venue for dumping the likes of Masson on his knees or backside should you get close enough. Alas, Masson has gone, Eric Mac, like all goalkeepers, believes he is Jimmy Greaves and Stubbo is under the impression he can play like Beckenbauer. An entertaining hour and diversion before the real thing tomorrow.

Over at the Forest they have their same routine. Some years ago, so Sammy Chapman, their centre half told us one night, Gentleman Jim Baxter, Slim Jim who was drinking Nottingham dry to pass the time of his dreary and unproductive stay at the City Ground away, would reign supreme on Friday morning. "Nobody went near him," Sammy said, and not just because his breath

142

wreaked of freshly partaken whisky. "He would nominate a nutmeg from 20 yards and that was that. The genius of the man."

Saturday, March 29

The slow motion, fat boy returns. In the worst dreams it is slow motion that prevents us from reaching our destination, the safe harbour from bad things and people chasing behind. Today, it is reverse motion and a ten ton slab of concrete that is hindering progress; that is control like a baby elephant. There are just over 8,105 at Meadow Lane to see Cardiff City and 8,104 of those are baying for my blood; Flash had set up a reasonable chance with a neat dribble and cut back from the byline but the finish was scuffed like a Sunday afternoon amateur. It is the universal and unchallenged law of football elasticity, like the laws of gravity and Boyle's Law and countless other laws of physics that I learned to say at school but know sod all about, that the harder you try to dig yourself out of the hole, the deeper it gets. The leaden feet, opponents moving twice the speed of light to close down. The ball is a balloon when it comes to control; like a medicine ball when it comes to passing. Some players get through these matches, others wilt. Hello Mr Wilt. Trouble is, when you are local to the club, everyone seems to know your social life and your love life. Since I don't have a latter, the terrace wags can concentrate on the former. There is plenty of scope for wit and repartee. Doyens of the art can hit a spot several inches below the belt from 100 yards without even trying.

Boos at the half-time whistle and Jimmy tells me to get in the bath. Public shame, private tears and I'm gone from the ground by 4 o'clock. On the radio, Colin Slater is saying the crowd behaved disgracefully. But they pay their money. It gets no better, apparently, and Cardiff return to the valleys 2-0 winners.

It has been the worst day of my life. And at home granddad is so worried for me. His haunted look tells me he no longer worries for himself. He is beyond it.

Wednesday, April 2

A run out at centre half for the reserves at Meadow Lane has restored confidence but tonight, at The Hawthorns, it is back in the midfield minefield. Stumped up another £20 fine for being late for training the other day. A blizzard in the first half against West Bromwich then a whirlwind of goals in the second. Tony Brown, Len Cantello, going in from all angles. Four-nil down and then I sneaked a late goal, deflected off the skidding surface. Even that passed without the joy of celebration. All in all, it has not been the best of weeks.

Saturday, April 12

Three games to go and Jimmy knows we need a few points in the bag to be certain of safety. A draw with Forest a couple of weeks ago, Clough's first Nottingham derby, has been the only respite from defeat. We are a wee bit too close for comfort, eh. In the afternoon heatwave on the south coast at Fratton Park, there are nine good men and true behind the ball, defying the Pompey chimes; Flash on the right with four across the middle and The Claw dropping deep with only Scanny making a token effort up front. "Jesus Christ, Ian, give him the fucking ball," Jimmy is shouting frantically from the dugout. The Bolt is on the half-way line and with no options forward, he has turned around and seen Stubbo and Neddy but it is Eric Mac, 50 yards further back, to whom Jimmy wants him to release the pass. There are ten minutes gone and the pattern of play for the next eighty has been set. The Portsmouth fans are livid but Jimmy is unrepentant. Having bored them rigid for most of the match Scanny snatches a goal at the death; from nothing, our first real attack. And then Camara, who has done nothing previously, gets a lucky break away from Ray down the right and drags one back for their big Went to bludgeon an equaliser with the last kick of the game. Jimmy gets his point after all.

In the bath later, Super Scanny is full of himself. He has saved us from relegation single-handedly. His goals have kept us up, etc, etc. Probey and Neddy beg to differ and before long, the Scot not so deep inside him has smashed a bottle on the huge brick bath. It is an unnecessary and superfluous gesture. The prima donna has had his say, though, and he is left to fantasize about his own worth alone in the tepid but turd-free water.

Saturday, April 19

There have not been enough bottle tops for Jimmy to use to explain the way Manchester United are going to play against us today. They only need a point to be champions, worthy ones at that and deserve their immediate return to

the First Division. Don Revie is at Meadow Lane to consider young talent for the England Under-21 team but the prospect that his eyes will rest upon me for any given amount of time belongs on Fantasy Island along with Scanny. Meadow Lane has been invaded by United fans; not since Boxing Day when Forest played there has the Spion Kop been so bursting with the ebb and flow of a vibrant red and white sea of celebration. As a rule, you can pick out the fans individually on that particular terracing but as we run out before kick-off, they are climbing up the pylons and supporting legs of the white wooden half-time scoreboard. Kicking against this patchwork is mesmerizing, as if the Mancunian masses are willing our every foray towards Alex Stepney's goal

Note the enthusiastic applause as Steve James leads out promoted Manchester United - Sammy McIlroy, with hair before he took the Northern Ireland manager's job, is lagging two places behind.

Man-to-man marking the San Marino way.
Stuart Pearson is close to scoring. McVay (left) is nowhere near to
preventing him. The dynamic Steve Carter (second left) is in the
thick of the action as always.

back with a magnetic force borrowed from the Stretford
End. If they had seen him spilling his Bacardi at the
Hilton in March, they surely would have turned up the
power on their impenetrable gravity shield. No matter, by
the interval, Mr Slow Motion is on the pitch and United
are 2-0 ahead. Eric Mac didn't get the best of cover but
two soft headers from Stewart Houston and Brian
Greenhoff trickle in. Brindley and me are close on hand,
alert and nose-picking as usual, as both efforts dawdle
across the line. "Fucking hell, McVay, this could be a
rout, lad," Billy blusters with a nervous mocking tone.

But it is not. Probey muscles in between James and
Houston to pull one back and the United hordes, now
behind us, are less disruptive. Stepney, out of the blue,

147

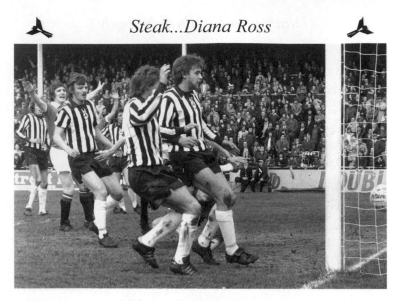

Brindley raises his hand in celebration as Brian Greenhoff's header
gently crosses the line to make it 2-0 to United.
"I have found one McVay!" he exclaims. He means a bogey. Nose-
picking while the opposition ran riot in the penalty area was so
much fun and obligatory at the Lane.

makes a brilliant save from Flash and Scanny wastes a
great chance. Now every tackle hits the mark. The
arrogant, highly-paid bastards are not superhuman after
all. Suitably up for it, The Claw polishes off Probey's
good work to make it 2-2. Denis would have been proud
of you Kevin.

You would have thought the point and the Second
Division title would have pleased the United fans.
Instead, they take to the pitch, devouring the goalposts,
gouging out huge lumps of Peter's beloved grass and
kicking in the glass above our dressing room beneath the
Main Stand. For one moment, there is a real danger of the
yobs breaking in. Stubbo, who was sent scurrying for

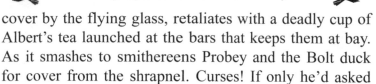

cover by the flying glass, retaliates with a deadly cup of Albert's tea launched at the bars that keeps them at bay. As it smashes to smithereens Probey and the Bolt duck for cover from the shrapnel. Curses! If only he'd asked the bastards to drink it.

Then sheer farce as the gaffer dashes into Jack's treatment room and emerges with a scalpel, a weapon victorious in defeating the hardest of meanest bunions but untried in this particular theatre of war. "Come on you fucking bastards, let's have you," he rants, gliding rapidly through the dressing room brandishing the tiny scalpel at the United mob. Out into the corridor, towards the players' tunnel with Brindley and Probey doubled up in guffaws and Jack making conciliatory remarks to stop him. "Gaffer, don't do it boss," they shout but it's lost in uncontrollable fits of laughter reverberating around the dressing room. In the darkest hours, laughter prevails. Stubbo rallies himself to support Jimmy and the two of them are thwarted by several boys in blue on guard at the end of the tunnel. They will never realise just how close they were brushing with death and Scalpel Sirrel of the Gorbals this afternoon.

Thursday, April 24

They had taken granddad to hospital last week. He knew he would never be returning home. The cancer destroyed his body and the surgeons, playing God, destroyed his face and final months on this earth.

Monday, April 28

Jack had been in charge at sunny Oxford on Saturday with the gaffer away on a mystery mission, the first time any of us could remember him missing a first team game. A 2-1 win at the Manor Ground - The Claw gets two - and we finish 14th in the Second Division - two places and two points above the Forest. This is good. "Jack tells me you were a credit on Saturday. It means a lot, eh, to our supporters. So well done eh." And David, you are in the reserves on Wednesday. There is a backlog of games to pull in. Which means another night out in the Stiffs living dangerously if Smithy forgets to apply his pile cream at half time. "Bloody hell Jack, my arse is on fire," he shouted across the mercifully empty terracing of Ayresome Park last week. "I've forgot the fucking cream." Jack: "You bloody dirty little sod, Smithy." And off Jack went, back to the dressing room and fetched the tube, the contents of which Smithy smoothed into his inflamed bowels before the main stand with his shorts and jock strap rolled down to his knees. One of the truly great sporting pictures of 1975. Memo diary: Must see more of Sue Goodband - or less if she has anything to do with it!

Friday, May 2

A new contract. £60 per week. Two years after leaving school for £25 a week it is difficult to refuse. Paul says ask for more but then he thought that man didn't land on the moon. He might be right after all. An audience with

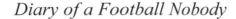

Jimmy is required, a trip into his office to discuss matters that frequently brings surprises. First you have to squirm your way through what passes for Ronnie's office, adjacent to Jimmy's. Inside, there is an almost Dickensian feel to the place; a dark and broody place, dimly lit by a shaft of light that struggles through a narrow slit of a window of frosted glass set in the Main Stand; the incongruity of dark oak and plasterboard décor and a couple of chairs and a cheap desk. Add the big stuffed bear and it is Steptoe's front room. Many have passed this way before. On some mornings, Jack has revealed, he sits in his chair and hears the footsteps of latecomers taking the alternative route to the dressing room, over the terraces and in through the players' tunnel to avoid detection. "Jackson, that's Carter. Fine the little bastard," he would tell Jack. And he was seldom wrong - and even when he was, he was right of course, boss.

"I didnay ask you take on a mortage," he informs me when I tried a lamentable bluff for a bit more. "You want to buy a car and a house, that's your decision." The senior pros are on about £80 so £60 is a good offer. For another couple of years, the deal is sealed. Dennis Marshall will draw up the contract next week.

Friday, May 9

The Russians are coming; Dynamo Minsk in a friendly at Meadow Lane. Last night we have beaten Forest 1-0 in the County Cup and then, of much greater significance, hammered them in boat races and general

drinking in the TBI. Tonight, the sun continues to shine as it has done for weeks now. The game is a 4-4 draw although how we manage to end up equal is beyond me. Perhaps sensing that I was swung to socialism in a former life and persuaded their goalkeeper to throw one of my crosses into his goal. But in the centre of their midfield was a little bald-headed chap, possibly KGB-trained, whose distribution was immaculate. It was a friendly, admittedly, but once he got hold of the ball, nobody could dispossess him. A former Russian international, most of us felt humble in his company, a gifted player who was a joy to watch, which is exactly what we did for most of the 90 minutes. And then the penalties, and poor old Arthur, who has not been in Jimmy's best books, misses one - deliberately perhaps to annoy the gaffer. So the Russians win and Jimmy goes absolutely beserk. Totally lost it, especially after we exchange shirts at the final whistle. The black and white stripes for white v-neck army issue material with blue trim - and my initials. Ochen Harashow! I try to show off my Russian A level oral to the opposition that my old teacher said sounded like a Siberian peasant on drugs. Their thoughts, though, are of a different oral examination preoccupied as they are by some of the more well endowed cleavages of the regulars of the Centenary Bar and 99 who are displaying their hefty assets to good effect. A surreal evening ends up in the Trent Bridge Inn with Harry Latchman, the Notts off-spinner talking of ice and its use as a sexual stimulant. Sublime, Harry. Dosvidanya.

Sunday, May 11

From the sublime to the ridiculous. Our close season tour of Gibraltar has begun with Probey having drunk a bottle of whisky on the plane from London Airport. On the balcony of the Rock Hotel (named after the huge granite thing looming over it) Jimmy is holding court, explaining why he blew his top after the Minsk game. He lays down the law, incensed that we had the temerity to consider swapping shirts without permission of the club and Jolly Jack. "They cost money, not your money, eh." In future we must ask first. Probey, equally incensed, says he will offer to pay for the cost of the fucking shirt. Slurs it a hundred times. "That's not the point, Eric son," Jimmy is slightly placatory, maybe realising there could be revolt in the ranks. In fact, it is close. The senior pros don't need this sort of discipline but Brindley for one is too busy ensuring Probey doesn't keel over backwards and over the balcony onto the rocks beneath in some sort of ghastly death sequence from a Hitchcock film.

Sunday, May 18

We return having won the Rock Trophy, somehow beating Fulham over two legs. Clearly Busby and Co managed to drink more than us during the week. Not more than Brindley, Stubbs and Probert, surely. Mission Impossible. We return having been regaled by Ralph Sweet, one of the County directors, and his Olympic medals for high diving during the war - or was it after. Nice one Ralphie - have you met Scanny. We are indebted

Rocking all over the world - well, Gibraltar was a start anyway.
Fulham, beaten in the FA Cup Final a few weeks earlier, were to
lose an even more prestigious piece of silverware, The Rock
Trophy. Defeated over two legs by Notts County's finest, the
'Suffern Pufters' also came second in the drinking contest.

Back Row: Tristan Benjamin, McVay, Ian Bolton, Eric McManus,
Billy Brindley, Kevin Randall, Jimmy Sirrel.
Front row: Mick Vinter, Pedro Richards, Brian Stubbs, David
Needham, Eric Probert, Steve Carter.

to the RAF for allowing us to train on their parade and give us a sporting chance in a cricket match when not one of us could see the ball least of all stand up and take guard. We also return indebted to Jimmy for tales of his days in the Merchant Navy when men were men, sailors were not hello sailors and sharks infested every stretch of water in which he sailed. And when Jimmy went out a little from the hotel beach and swam on his back, there was Brindley and Probey, Jimmy's nose protruding out of the water, running around asking everyone to clear the sand. "Just when you thought it was safe to go back in the water," they proclaimed in the midday sun having consumed at least seven pints of Watney's Red barrel in the 'Village Pub' that morning.

Wednesday, May 28

Desperately trying to look smart tonight for a presentation evening at the Sherwood Rooms. Dougie Ward, an old friend of granddad's, has asked me to help out for Clifton All Whites, the football team of my teens and one that has dominated Nottingham youth football for years. Viv and Pete Wells, both former players, have agreed. Should have known giving pints of lager to Wellsy, veteran of The Grey Mare, Clifton Estate's roughest, toughest, meanest and lowest form of life pub, would be like throwing strawberries to pigs. The lad has hollow legs. Viv sticks to rum and pep. A fulfilling evening, as if giving something back and at least the bunch of under 10s, 11s and 12s really do believe we are stars in the way they ask for autographs. Not yet tainted with the cynic

inside us all. Leeds are playing in the European Cup final and Lorimer has put them ahead against Bayern Munich in Paris. It's a brilliant volley even if it is not a welcome sentiment watching the final on television upstairs on the balcony of the Sherwood Rooms. Leeds are frowned upon as either being too successful, too dirty or treating badly 'our Cloughie' at Elland Road. At any rate the lager has gripped Wells and me. Lorimer's goal is ruled offside

Only a saying was Give Peace A Chance.
After that, Viv Anderson and Peter Wells (on the left) were to get their chances in the Nottingham Forest first team. Dougie Ward (centre) seems pleased that he has lost his glasses to some berk on his left, or maybe he's just glad that Leeds United have been beaten by Bayern Munich in the European Cup Final on the same night. I'm afraid that a large quantity of alcohol was abused during the making of this picture.

and Bayern score two late, spawny goals. The Clough faction is happy. I am pissed. Wells is stone cold sober. Viv has disappeared. Bastard German efficiency.

Monday, June 9

Natalie walks on this earth for the first time. Nick Drake no longer can. The sun, that never ceases to glow every day and long night this summer, ain't gonna shine any more on the old lad now he's topped himself.

Saturday, June 21

So what did you do on holiday this year boss? A week in the Lakes and a week in a caravan with Smithy and some of his dodgy mates at Skeggy. The world is my lobster, Billy. Clunk, off the bar stool at the Pavilion Club on North Shore. West Indies beat Australia in the cricket World Cup final late today. Brilliant game.

Saturday, July 5

Connors loses to Ashe. Rosewall avenged. A deserving defeat for that letter from Mom in his sock. Get a grip, Jimbo.

Wednesday, July 9

Scanny exhibits signs that he has returned to Planet Earth on our first day back. His passage has been expedited by

his latest four-wheel acquisition - a 1600RS Escort. Red of course, twin camshaft. Not a car to tangle with, he reckons. Especially with Scanny, who hasn't passed his test, behind the wheel.

Tuesday, July 29

The pre-season slog is almost over. Defeats at Arsenal's and Aston Vanilla's training grounds have not deterred Jimmy for the new season. A couple of new faces including Frankie 'Do Not Forsake Me, Oh My Darling' Lane from Liverpool Reserves. Eternally optimistic Scouser who is destined for Notts County Reserves as a goalkeeper. Great touch with his feet as a centre forward in five-a-sides; not too sure about his handling in his chosen position as yet but he has been embraced as one of the drinking fraternity who stands his round. Little else matters - at least until the pressure is on and season starts. There is a confidence in the camp, definitely. Having taken this side from the bottom of the Fourth Division to mid-table in the Second, it could be time to move on. The gaffer believes in it and with the likes of Vint, the Bolt and Pedro coming through, there is a younger edge that blends in with the more mature furniture of Brindley, Bradd, Needham and Stubbs. Well, that's what Terry Bowles, the Evening Post reporter, wrote last week.

Friday, August 8

The afternoon blazing heat has induced apathy and sleep, interrupted by a phone call from the office. The friendly

Notts County FC 1975/76 season.
Blow-dried and pristine, just out of the shower on parade for pre-season photographs. Jimmy Sirrel's timeless suit is more fashionable today than it ever was when it adorned his body. Tristan Benjamin's Afro (Back row, centre) was in its infancy before it grew to obscure the County Road stand and the sun in subsequent team photos.

at Kettering Town tomorrow has been called off because their stand has been torched by vandals. Amazing how the prospect of an unexpected day off can galvanise previously idle minds and ambitions. Like a holiday when the school was being used as a polling station for elections, school's out and the bush telegraph is working as efficiently as ever. Brindley has rounded up a number of willing volunteers for the drinking squad - that is most of the first team that would have played tomorrow - and arranged to meet in the Flying Horse tonight. By the time we rendezvous, the old pub has been re-named the Flying

Magpie - aka Brindley on large Bacardi and Cokes. The night that began badly gets worse and descends into notoriety when those who are remaining - can't recall who - are asked to leave a party in the posher part of Wollaton at three in the morning. Without wings and Bacardi to sustain him, the Flying Brindley had crashed on terra firma long before.

Saturday, August 9

Saturday morning is not Saturday morning without Tiswas and the Phantom Flam Flinger plus the added bonus of an almighty thud in the cranium and a nauseous feeling in the pit of the stomach. The condition is not helped by another bloody phone call from Meadow Lane. Dennis Marshall rings to say the game is on after all. The hoax caller yesterday had rang to say that the Kettering stand had burned down but nobody bothered to check out its validity. A jolly good jape, indeed, but Billy, the Flying Magpie just a few joyous hours before, does not appreciate the humour. The colour of his jowls - varying like a chameleon from a pallid shade of death in the dazzling sunshine outside the ground where we gathered later in the morning to the camouflage sickly green to match the velour trim in the hotel where we forced down poached eggs on toast - give the game away. He chews violently, vigorously on spearmint gum, breaking out in a sweat at the perpetual motion of his jaws. I almost feel better seeing him suffer - almost, but not quite. "Oxygen, McVay," he gasps as another

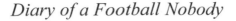

young pretender to part-time fame trying to impress Derek Doogan, the new manager of the Southern League side, mounts a mazy dribble against our right back who would prefer to have been left back in the dressing room. "I canne take much more, Macca." The game is five minutes old and pure spirit is pouring from every orifice known to man. "Look at that fucking Bradd. He's not moved once the big lazy bastard. BRADDY, yes you fucking bastard, are you going to start today? Look at him, clocking a deaf un, pretending he can't hear the gaffer. There's pigeon shit on your head, you lazy bastard." And so a variation on a theme of words continued for ten minutes. Beat the Clock contestants, you have ten seconds to re-arrange these words into a well known phrase. Bradd, Lazy, Bastard, Fucking. Off you go. Reports of the Kettering main stand's demise were clearly premature. It is looking in remarkably rude health considering it was the victim of a recent arson attack and it offers shade from the unrelenting sunshine for one half of the pitch nearest its corrugated roof. Sadly, it is not for Brindley or me; the right side but the wrong side of team selection today. Professional pride is a great motivation, especially when you are playing non-league players who have a point to prove - either failed apprentices, discarded young pros on free transfers or a teenager hoping to be spotted and take your place in the pro ranks. Having floundered like two sweating hippos in the afternoon heatwave for 20 minutes, class finally tells. We hammer them 4-3! Did we need a drink after that.

Monday, August 18

A new season has just begun with a 2-1 win at Charlton Athletic on Saturday. And a life has ended today. Grandma, Rose Anna, died after just a couple of days in hospital. The will to live gone, a life of pain and struggle in recent years is over.

Friday, August 22

"Jesus, we played on with broken legs." Brindley, the Six Dollar Man who has been rebuilt more times than Steve Austin, is reminding me of my duties. On Tuesday night a docker from London's East End clobbered me nearly across the capital after catching my ankle at Brisbane Road. Since that 1-1 draw, I have been hobbling all week, receiving treatment but convincing nobody that I am not fit to play against Southampton tomorrow. "It's in your mind David, son," Jack, ever patient, tells me. I know Jack, and that's the problem because it's the same bloody ankle that went against Hull. "Let's have him out on the pitch Jackson," Jimmy says after another morning on the treatment table. There is Jack, me and the gaffer on the halfway line; the sun is out and all is well with the world - except this strapped-up ankle.

"Jack, breenge a couple of balls," and Jack dutifully drills in a pass to feet. "Give it me son," Jimmy is calling for the ball about 20 yards away. "Now chase that, go, go, go." Jimmy has knocked an impossible pass to the edge of the penalty box and I retrieve it, turn tenderly on the

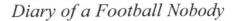

bad ankle and sprint back towards Jimmy. Before I get there, he is walking away to the tunnel. "Jesus Christ, Jackson, that boy is fit. Get him strapped up for tomorrow, eh!" Jack follows him obediently down the tunnel, laughing. The amazing healing powers of Doctor Sirrel have triumphed once again.

Saturday, August 23

The gaffer, as always, is right. A half decent game in a 0-0 draw with Southampton and the ankle was fine. Brindley is visiting his mum and dad after the game. A short walk over Iremonger Bridge to their terraced house in The Meadows. Charlie, his dad, welcomes us with a bottle of beer each and a chat about my game and Billy's. The warmth in the front room of the two-up, two-down property is intoxicating. Images of his mum, like all Meadows' mums, scrubbing the steps and tipping out the dirty water down the drain. Grandma was cremated yesterday. In between treatment and fitness tests there was her funeral. They are demolishing The Meadows now. The finality of life, the end of eras is enveloping me tonight like winter smog.

Friday, August 29

A meeting of opposites in the café at Debenhams department store this afternoon. Dave Serella, Robbo, O'Neill and Viv are there with The Claw, Flash and Scanny. The red half of the city mixing with the black and white but talking with the

enemy is acceptable on the eve of the Nottingham derby. Huge Johns, the legendary Star Soccer commentator, "Well, it's a game of two halves, Billy" resides at the Posthouse with the rest of us tonight. The derby tomorrow, no McKenzie but Terry Curran, a right winger signed by Clough for £75,000, could prove our nemesis. Switching to the left side of midfield, Jimmy has told me to back-track and double-up with Ray, not to leave him exposed. "Aye, and you must get forward, too, David." Yes boss.

Saturday, August 30

"Owt tide, owt tide," Ray's dulcet Irish tones tell me to force Curran wide. "Weltun, David," are Ray's sugar cubes for the puzzled pit pony that is charging up and down the left flank like a demented beast. A rare spark of creation at last, a deep cross that Braddy heads back beyond John Middleton before Chapman, the bastard, recovers to clear it off the line. But this is our season, our derby and Scanny gets away, again on the left, and another far post cross and Braddy buries it this time. Middleton, Chapman on their knees. 1-0, 89th minute. Fourth in the league. More sugar cubes, please. How will Huge and Billy see this one tomorrow? A game of one minute, maybe. But what a minute.

Wednesday, September 3

Note to diary: I am starting to laugh out loud at Terry Wogan. The pills and a darkened room nurse. Quickly.

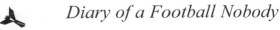

Try as he might, Liam O'Kane (no.4) is unable to defy gravity under the weight of his sideburns. Meanwhile, Sammy Chapman, the Forest centre-half, tries to terminate what had been a pretty crap and brief love life with an old-fashioned boot to the goolies.

Luckily, I have turned the other cheek, bedazzled by Viv Anderson's perm. Les Bradd, who scored the only goal of the game in the 89th minute, is second right.

Chapman (second left) is on his knees after Bradd's late winner. John Middleton, the Forest goalkeeper, sits it out while the black and white stripes from the left are Carter, McVay, Probert, Bolton and Stubbs.

Tuesday, September 9

Another hot, sultry night at the end of this remarkable summer and Sunderland are at Meadow Lane in the League Cup. The Bolt, a streaky six foot of flesh, no flab, no muscle, had displeased Towers of Sunderland who, having chinned him, was sent off along with his victim in the first half. Probey misses a penalty but a 2-1 win in an invigorating, unyielding cup-tie atmosphere.

Thursday, September 11

Practice match (shock, horror) on Meadow Lane after overnight rain and Peter has more reason to be awkward and grumpy. "Why can't they use the flaming training ground, that's what it's there for," is the sound logic he espouses in a fairly convincing argument. It has fallen, not surprisingly, on deaf ears once again. Jimmy is listening intently elsewhere in his ramshackle office this morning. Eventually he emerges down the tunnel and walks around the running track to the far side of the pitch, beneath the County Road stand. "We have plucked a fucking peach," he announces, breaking out in a huge grin as he stops the meandering game with a peep of that whistle. "Leeds fucking United away in the next round. A fucking peach, eh, Jackson. Now they can play, eh. Boy can they play. But so can we, Jackson. And we can stop them. Aye, we can stop them all right," and he walks away, joy uncontained at the thought of trying to do just that - Hunter, Bremner, Reaney, Lorimer, Clarke, the Gray brothers, Madeley and all. Shit!

Diary of a Football Nobody

Saturday, September 13

Stubbo is going spare at Bootham Crescent. "For fuck's sake, David, he's taking the piss out of you," and little Eric McMordie, the Northern Ireland now York City midfielder, probably was. A little nutmeg on the right and he was away and darting into our box before Stubbo gets across to concede a corner. It is a one-way conversation and it has the desired effect until, five minutes from time, he glides in at the far post to score with a header. "For fuck's sake David," Stubbo begins his rant again, saying I should have got up at the far post to stop him. By then, though, it is 2-0 and I have scored the second - a shot that was heading for the transport museum before it took a deflection and dipped over their goalkeeper. "Well, if he hadnay scored the second, perhaps we wouldnay have conceded their goal, eh Brian," Jimmy is in philosophical mood to calm the outraged Stubbs who is still determined to lay the blame at my feet, head actually, in the bath afterwards. We are top of the league and still he moans.

Sunday, September 14

The secret of my goal is out. "It hit the top of the telly and rebounded in," one of my greatest fans in the Clifton Bridge Inn explains tonight after seeing brief highlights on Yorkshire Television in the afternoon. It's good to have friends.

Steak...Diana Ross

YORK CITY

Match Number 5   Football League Division II
YORK CITY v NOTTS. COUNTY
Saturday 13th Sept., 1975   Kick off 3.00 p.m.

YORK CITY
(Maroon/White)

1 Graeme CRAWFORD
2 Cliff CALVERT
3 Derrick DOWNING
4 John WOODWARD
5 Barry SWALLOW
6 Chris TOPPING
7 Barry LYONS
8 Micky CAVE
9 Jimmy SEAL
10 Chris JONES
11 Eric McMORDIE
12

NOTTS. COUNTY
(Black/White)

1 Eric McMANUS
2 Peter RICHARDS
3 Ray O'BRIEN
4 Ian BOLTON
5 David NEEDHAM
6 Brian STUBBS
7 Steve CARTER
8 Eric PROBERT
9 Les BRADD
10 David McVAY
11 Ian SCANLON
12

OFFICIALS

Referee: J. WRENNALL
(Eccleston)

Linesmen:
Yellow Flag: R. FAIRLEY
(Spennymoor)
Red Flag: N. RILEY
(Bolton)

PRICE 10p

168

Diary of a Football Nobody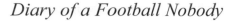

Left: Top of the world, top of the league and top of the telly.
All human life was there at Bootham Crescent. My goal against
York City was certainly worthy of the Twilight Zone or one of the
Tales of the Unexpected. The shot was destined to carry the ball
unerringly to its target - York Railway Museum, several miles
away - until it was gripped by a mystical force that guided it into
the back of the net. Perhaps it was aliens trying to kidnap Jimmy
before their tractor beam went haywire.

Saturday, September 27

After a 2-0 win at Hull City on Tuesday night, we are on
top of the world, unbeaten in nine league and cup games
and the BBC have paid a visit. Even Bob Wilson on
Football Focus manages not to talk about Arsenal for 10
seconds and gives us a mention. After the white of
England shirts at Boothferry Park, Jimmy has chosen a
new away strip for the game at Sunderland, who are
second, one point behind us. Yellow shirts with a huge,
thick vertical green band down the middle; the stuff of
television tuning on Mars. The gaffer's sartorial elegance
is a subject of debate that lightens the tension before kick-
off. Neddy thinks Jolly Jack has found a job lot of cast-
off Norwich shirts and green paint to save a few bob.

It is Roker with nearly 30,000 inside but the roar is
muted until two minutes before half time when Vic
Halom barges into Eric Mac. It's a simple up and under
he should hold on to but Halom has knocked him in the
air, the ball is loose and it's 'Pop' Robson and one bastard
nil just when we didn't need it. There is no way back.
Torrential rain, a sagging new kit and the vertical hold has
slipped. 4-0.

Monday, September 29

Jimmy has told Jack, who then whispers it to us long after the gaffer has gone home, that the yellow penguin outfits will never be seen again. It's back to the drawing board - we fear the worst.

Wednesday, October 8

It is nights like these that restore faith in it all; the thin man returns at Elland Road, bloody Elland Road. What a ground, billiard ball playing surface and changing rooms with tiles in the bath. New tiles, that is. Clean tiles. And proper soap that doesn't smell of disinfectant. Brindley, who was playing for the reserves at Doncaster last night, is named at right back. With Ray struggling, Pedro moves to left back. "This is what it's all about, Macca," Billy is geeing us all up but there is massive nervous tension. And not only because we almost were spotted smuggling the Teasmaid out of the Posthouse near Leeds in the afternoon. It is a long way from Kettering and Belle Vue and Brindley, strapped up, aching, limping and knackered from the previous night's exertions, is relying on me to help him with Eddie Gray. And he isn't joking.

"Show him the line, son, we'll be all right" but then there is only his brother Frank, younger and nimbler down the left, to worry about. For 45 minutes it is working. Leeds, oozing class and eleven internationals, are patient, knock it about but Braddy has a half chance in the air. We are in with a shout. We sense it. Jimmy tells us the game is there to be won at half-time. And he is

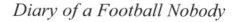

right. Again. It is Super Notts according to over 5,000 fans who have travelled up the M1; Bradd then Scanny go close, Scanny hits the post and then, on the end of a cross, he heads past Harvey for 1-0. Super Notts, indeed, and Super Scan, certainly. The rest is a blur, running smoothly, uninterrupted and slimly on the green baize. A final flurry from Reaney just wide with a right foot shot, a kick on the ankle from Bremner because it was there and he couldn't resist it and another shimmy and run from Eddie Gray runs into Brindley's size nines.

The better side has won on the night and we are delirious. Jimmy, ecstatic. And in the aftermath of victory, a drink offered by Norman Hunter in the players' bar, serving behind the hatch and first to shake our hands as we enter. The champagne back in Nottingham could not compare. What it's all about Billy, eh.

Footnote: Two weeks later Jimmy Sirrel departed Meadow Lane and was appointed manager of Sheffield United, then bottom of the First Division. Ronnie Fenton was named team manager of Notts County.

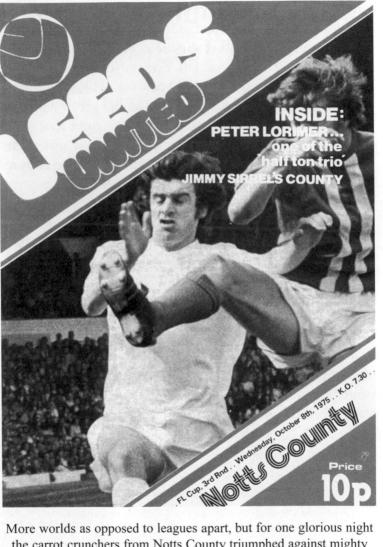

More worlds as opposed to leagues apart, but for one glorious night
the carrot crunchers from Notts County triumphed against mighty
Leeds United in the People's Republic of West Yorkshire.
But Norman Hunter beat us all to the bar!

Further Round the bend beyond Meadow Lane

THE MANAGEMENT:

JIMMY SIRREL: Jimmy did not enjoy his time with Sheffield United and returned to Notts, replacing Ronnie Fenton in October 1978. His first task was to rescue me from Torquay United, a smashing, family club, to which I had been banished on a month's loan. Ronnie couldn't find a more remote point on the map and I don't think the Faroe Islands were accepting overseas players then. Jimmy enjoyed his 80th birthday in the company of former players, friends and invited guests at Meadow Lane in February 2002. He still lives in Burton Joyce, just to the east of Nottingham.

RONNIE FENTON: While Jimmy went to Sheffield, Ronnie endured an unhappy Notts County tenure although he was responsible for boldly going where no Notts manager had gone before, beyond Gibraltar on exotic tours to Magaluf and Kenya. He later crossed the River Trent and forged a successful alliance with Brian Clough at Nottingham Forest. Now retired from football, he can be seen at Notts County's reunion dinners.

JACK WHEELER: Jack went on to complete nearly 30 years service for the Magpies, seeing them reach the old First Division with Jimmy and Howard Wilkinson in

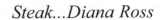
charge. When he retired, in 1985, Jack Dunnett took him into his office and offered him his thanks for giving blood, sweat and tears to the club - and a form on how to apply for disability benefit because of his dodgy hips that had become an occupational hazard sitting in wet and windy dugouts from Scunthorpe to Hartlepool via Bournemouth. He was honoured by the Old Players' Association in 2001. Lives with Olga, his wife, in the clubhouse in Wollaton, near Nottingham, that he moved into when he first came to Notts with Tommy Lawton in 1957.

JACK DUNNETT: Jolly Jack - the nickname is facetious - ran a tight ship at Meadow Lane but his character references left a lot to be desired. When he sold the club in 1987 he had already served as President of the Football League but his ambition to be similarly acclaimed in the Football Association ultimately went unfulfilled. Became vice-chairman of Portsmouth in 1989 but fell from grace and off the football radar shortly afterwards.

FIRST XI (4-4-2):

ROY BROWN: Gradually lost his place to Eric McManus and moved on to Mansfield Town before taking up a post as manager of a sports centre in Watford. Reports of his demise were premature when the Nottingham Evening Post published a brief story noting his passing some two decades ago. Roy rang the news desk to take issue with his recent death. Happily, he remains stood six foot tall above ground today.

JOHN 'BILLY' BRINDLEY: One of the most enduring and endearing characters on the lower league circuit, Billy moved on to Gillingham but after two unhappy years in Kent he returned to Nottingham with his wife Catherine and two young children. Still falls off the piano to the strains of Great Balls of Fire as his encore at most social events in the Midlands area. He no longer sells eggs but cleaning materials as a high-powered sales executive for a multinational conglomerate. Allegedly.

DAVID NEEDHAM: 'Neddy' was destined for greater things and his move to Queen's Park Rangers then to Nottingham Forest, where he gained England B recognition, vindicated Jimmy's faith in his former apprentice's ability. Few ever fathomed what he did for a living to justify his lavish lifestyle and expensive cars. The same applies today. After the death of Arthur Mann, has been influential in fostering the spirit of the Old Players' Association and its organisation.

BRIAN STUBBS: Stubbsy never did move away from Meadow Lane even though many First Division managers cast an envious eye over his central defensive partnership with Needham. Was part of the squad that secured the Sirrel dream of taking the club from the bottom of the Fourth Division to the First. However, when Notts arrived there in 1981 he was denied his moment of glory and an appearance in the top flight by Wilkinson and Sirrel, who refused to pick him despite his outstanding service. Another character who still socialises in public houses

e River Trent in between work in the
ndustry.

BOB WORTHINGTON: Bob moved to Southend
United with his flash BMW 2002 but has remained in
touch with many of his friends and former colleagues in
Nottingham. Like Neddy, plays a big part in the Old
Players' Association even though he upped sticks from
near Halifax and moved to France last year.

JON NIXON: Even Dwight Yorke and Jack Nicklaus
combined could not match his impressive club selection.
Peterborough United and Shrewsbury Town were among
those that followed for Nixo after Meadow Lane. In
retirement he joined Needham in a car number plate
business venture. Currently involved in hi-tech and
computer software. I think.

DON MASSON: Not for good reason, Masson is
regarded as the greatest County player of all time,
certainly by a generation who cannot recall Tommy
Lawton's heady days at the club. Leading Scotland in the
1978 World Cup Finals was perhaps his finest hour,
although many would say that his rehabilitation after the
tragic death of his wife Margaret should take precedence.
Admits to being a changed person from his off-days as
Masson the Miserable in the County dressing room. The
beers are free during meetings of former players
convened regularly at the hotel he owns near Trent
Bridge.

ERIC PROBERT: Probey eventually left Notts in the mid-1970s with a flock of albatrosses (or whatever a group of the gathered same is called) hanging around his neck. He took over a pub near Boroughbridge and briefly appeared for Darlington as the decade came to a close.

ARTHUR MANN: Never really received the credit he deserved at Meadow Lane but went on, with Alan Buckley, to achieve greater things in a coaching capacity with Grimsby Town and West Bromwich Albion. When Arthur died in 1999, a result of a tragic accident with a fork-lift truck in a delivery yard of his employers, there were several football clubs represented by hundreds of players, past and present, young and old, whose lives he had touched briefly. A fitting tribute to a lovely bloke and, above all, devoted family man.

LES BRADD: The Big Bomber was still scoring goals after County, mainly for Wigan Athletic, where with Larry Lloyd, the former non-league club gained promotion from the old Fourth Division. In retirement, Les joined the County 75 lottery staff at Meadow Lane then became part of the Forest commercial staff, a position he holds to this day.

KEVIN RANDALL: The Claw continued to defy age and rubber legs as a forward with Mansfield Town, with whom he managed one more promotion while bankrupting the north Notts club by his obsession with tubes of Deep Heat, the contents of which he would immerse himself in from head to toe before kick off. "There he goes, down the Time

Tunnel," colleagues opined and he would re-emerge on the pitch looking pallid (that was the Deep Heat) but running around as if his bollocks were on fire (see previous parenthesis). Still involved in the game as a scout for Sheffield United, although has not, as yet, confronted Denis Law for his autograph. Sad old git.

Substitute:

TRISTAN BENJAMIN: Benjy's hair blossomed far more freely than his conversation but the quiet man of Meadow Lane emerged as one of the most consistent defenders as the club secured promotion to the First Division. One of several brothers with a fine footballing tradition, he played briefly for Chesterfield before pursuing a career as a social worker.

STIFFS (4-4-2):

ERIC MCMANUS: A move to Stoke City when in the prime of his form did not auger well for Eric. He suffered a severe elbow injury at the Victoria Road and moved on to Bradford City before finishing his career with Tranmere Rovers. Latterly involved in coaching with Coventry City and Derby County.

PEDRO RICHARDS: After ten years service with the club, Pedro was granted a testimonial season which, considering that the Notts side was in considerable decline at the time, was not able to fulfil expectations. Rather like Pedro's own playing career. A talent that never reached its true potential. He remained in The Meadows to which he came as a young Spanish-speaking schoolboy aged 11 until his untimely death, aged 45, at Christmas, 2001.

IAN BOLTON: After a loan spell at Lincoln City, the Bolt finally departed Meadow Lane to join Graham Taylor's Watford. His lightning pace, thunderous shot and the Benson and Hedges smokescreen that followed him around Vicarage Road were part of the scenery as Taylor's team swept from the Fourth to the First Division as swiftly as the Bolt could light up twenty filter tips.

PAUL 'SAMMY' DYER: Sammy rode off into the sunset in his Bedford van, never to be seen again. Well apart from four seasons with Colchester United. Same thing, really.

RAY O'BRIEN: Became a part of the County folklore with his left-footed free kicks and indecipherable accent. Lives and works in the county while he still helps to manage Arnold Town, a local non-league side, along with Brindley.

STEVE CARTER: They never did get Carter, but then Flash was always there to save the world, or at least his own skin, out on the right wing. Continued to 'corkscrew' full backs for Derby County and Bournemouth. Later returned to Great Yarmouth to run the family whelk stall, he alleged.

DAVE SMITH: His move to Torquay United signalled the end for Mike Green, the manager who took me on

loan there. Mike, one of the nicest blokes in football, never stood a chance once Smithy and his underpants hit Plainmoor. Remained on the south coast in the pub trade, in which he is involved today somewhere near Plymouth.

EDDIE CLIFF: From Tranmere to Chicago and then back to Rochdale. That was Eddie's itinerary after Meadow Lane. Never did find out if he joined the teaching ranks. Their gain, football's loss I suppose.

IAN SCANLON: What can you say about Scan the Man. Upset at being dropped by Ronnie one New Year's Day, he went AWOL from the team coach at Carlisle, completing an unusual Scottish journey that took him over Hadrian's Wall heading north on a permanent basis. He re-surfaced confused but claiming that he was engaged to a heiress who stood to inherit millions of pounds. Ended up marrying a vicar's daughter from Wilford, a south Notts village, before returning happily to Scotland where he played for Aberdeen.

MICK VINTER: Sold for a club record fee of £150,000 to Wrexham, Vint continued to score goals at the Racecourse Ground and then the Manor Ground with Oxford United before he returned to the area with Mansfield Town. Still turning out locally.

GEOFF COLLIER: Never did see Geoff after Blackpool. Considering his drinking capacity and taste in women, probably for the best.

And last, but not least...

DAVID McBAY: Jimmy could get my name right when he felt in the mood. After Notts, I spent two marvellous years with Peterborough United before being shown the door on a free. Colin Murphy, then manager of Lincoln City, enticed me to join him at Sincil Bank and as anyone in football knows, two minutes spent in the company of Smurf is enough to drive anyone to drink (highly recommended) and the nearest deep canal (not so highly recommended having indulged in the latter). Rehabilitation came in the form of working as a football reporter then features writer for the Nottingham Evening Post for over a decade. Cured of the dreaded Smurf, I started work as a sports writer for The Times in the Midlands. A year or so into the job and Peter Taylor is appointed manager of Leicester City. And his first signing as director of football? Yep, Colin Murphy. Aaargh...the pills nurse, and quickly.